The ABCs of the UCC

(Revised) Article 2: Sales

Henry D. Gabriel
Linda J. Rusch

Amelia H. Boss
Editor
The ABCs of the UCC series

Defending Liberty
Pursuing Justice

Printed in the United States of America.

Library of Congress Cataloging-in-Publication Data

Gabriel, Henry D.
    The ABCs of the UCC. Revised Article 2. Sales / Henry D. Gabriel, Linda J. Rusch, Amelia H. Boss.
        p. cm.
    Includes bibliographical references.
    ISBN 1-59031-305-4 (pbk.)
    1. Sales—United States—States. I. Title: Article 2, Sales. II. Title: Sales. III. Rusch, Linda J., 1959- IV. Boss, Amelia H. V. American Bar Association. Section of Business Law. VI. Title.

    KF915.Z95G33 2004
    346.7307'2—dc22

                                                                2004007430

Cover design by Catharine Zaccarine.

Discounts are available for books ordered in bulk. Special consideration is given to state and local bars, CLE programs, and other bar-related organizations. Inquire at ABA Publishing, American Bar Association, 750 North Lake Shore Drive, Chicago, Illinois 60611.

08 07 06 05 04   5 4 3 2 1

CONTENTS

▼ CHAPTER 4

Contract Terms: Express and Implied Warranties   53

▼ CHAPTER 5

Offer, Acceptance, and Terms in the Hard Case: Section 2-207 and the Battle of the Forms

▼ CHAPTER 6

Contract Performance and Breach

▼ CHAPTER 7

Property Aspects of the Sales Transactions

▼ CHAPTER 8

FOREWORD

Over the half-century since it was enacted, the Uniform Commercial Code has become both an indispensable part of the study of law and an essential part of legal practice. Adopted by all fifty states, the Code has been hailed as one of the great products of American law. Its impact is by no means limited to the United States. The Code has become one of the United States's important exports: other nations have modeled their laws after our Uniform Commercial Code, and portions of the Code have been carried over into international instruments such as the United Nations Convention on the International Sale of Goods. Indeed, during an international conference at the United Nations in 1992 entitled "Uniform Commercial Law in the Twenty-First Century," repeated demands were heard for the creation of a Uniform International Commercial Code.

Despite the importance and impact of the Code, many practitioners and students find it difficult to master. Its provisions, followed by official comments, cross-references, and notes, often seem impenetrable. The problem stems from several sources.

First, as Grant Gilmore once observed, the Code sometimes appears to have been written in its own shorthand. The keys to deciphering that shorthand are frequently found in the definitions to the Code and are often found in an understanding of non-Code law.

Second, no single provision of the Code can truly be understood without an understanding of the other provisions of the Code and its overarching purposes, policies, and concepts. The interconnectedness of the Code's provisions and the importance of its often unarticulated policies require extended study for mastery.

Third, the Code, even on its own terms, does not purport to contain all the law there is on a particular subject; the Code may be uniform, but it is not comprehensive. The Code invites us to consult non-Code law to "fill in the gaps" in its coverage.

Last, the Uniform Commercial Code itself is not "law." Rather, the Code is adopted on a state-by-state basis; individual states may make nonuniform amendments during the adoption process, or state courts may interpret its provisions in a nonuniform manner, making it all the more difficult for the new practitioner or student to master.

This series of books, **The ABCs of the UCC**, a project of the Uniform Commercial Code Committee of the American Bar Association's Section of Business Law, is aimed at making the Code accessible to practitioner and student alike. Free of the footnotes and the extensive convoluted discussions that often accompany legal literature, each book is written to present the basic concepts and operation of the Code articles in a simple, straightforward manner. No attempt is made to treat the Code in an in-depth manner nor to cite to all possibly relevant authorities and cases. Rather, the goal is to provide the reader with the framework and basic knowledge of the Code necessary to orient the reader for future work or research. Thus, this series of books does not supplant, but rather complements, more intensive treatments of the subjects.

Each book in the series is devoted to one or two of the articles of the Code, yet they are intended to form a coherent whole, which, taken together, provides an overview of the Code in operation. Each book is written by a distinguished person in the field of commercial law who is considered an expert in the field by colleagues. The focus is on the uniform text of the Code: the text as adopted by the sponsors of the Code, the American Law Institute and the National Conference of Commissioners on Uniform State Laws. While the focus is on the uniform version, each book, where appropriate, points out important nonuniform amendments and divergent judicial treatment of the Code provisions.

In 1965, Grant Gilmore warned that the enactment of the Code and of Article 9 did not mark the end of the process of change and development in the field of commercial law. His comments were more perceptive than he could have realized. Today, as we move into the twenty-first century, the Code has undergone extensive revision and change. The well-advised practitioner or student realizes that the process of learning should be an ongoing one; the knowledge gained from reading this current series of ready reference books should nonetheless provide a firm foundation for supplementation in the future.

The Uniform Commercial Code Committee of the ABA's Section of Business Law welcomes the opportunity to provide these tools to the legal profession. We hope that you find this series of books useful for your needs.

Amelia H. Boss
Temple University School of Law
Editor

PREFACE

This primer explains the structure and methodology of Uniform Commercial Code Article 2 (Revised 2003) as it applies to typical sales transactions. Reading through this primer from beginning to end will provide the reader with a coherent approach to analyzing issues encountered in a sale of goods transaction. This primer may be used either as a review of issues previously encountered or as an introduction to Article 2. As with any explanation of law, however, careful reading of the statutory text and comments as well as consideration of decided cases are necessary in order to come to a full understanding of the area or to give competent advice to clients. The bibliography at the end of this book provides a starting point for further research.

Henry D. Gabriel
Linda J. Rusch

CHAPTER

ONE

INTRODUCTION

A. HISTORY OF ARTICLE 2

Article 2 is one of the ten substantive articles of the Uniform Commercial Code (UCC), developed by the National Conference of Commissioners on Uniform State Laws (NCCUSL) and the American Law Institute (ALI). These two bodies approve the draft statutes, which are then proposed to the states for adoption. Each state decides for itself whether to adopt a uniform law proposed in this manner. In addition, each state has the ability to make nonuniform amendments to the proposed statute, which will be effective in that particular state. Thus, the law may not be uniform across every state in the country. The uniform version proposed by NCCUSL and the ALI is referred to as the Official Version of the UCC (hereinafter the "Code"). As with every uniform law, however, a lawyer is foolish to rely upon the Official Version in contemplating issues in a real case. To determine the appropriate analysis of any issues a lawyer must consult the version as enacted in the state whose the law applies to the transaction.

Article 2 (Sales) was promulgated in 1957 and amended in 1958 and 1962. It did not arise out of whole cloth in the 1950s, however, but was built upon a common law foundation and upon another uniform act, the Uniform Sales Act, which in turn had its roots in the British Sale of Goods Act. The Uniform Sales Act, drafted in 1906 and revised in 1922, had been adopted in more than thirty states by the 1940s. When a state enacted Code Article 2, its version of the Uniform Sales Act was repealed.

The Official Version of Article 2 today is the 1962 version as amended by the 2003 amendments. The 1962 version was adopted in some form in all states except Louisiana. Article 2 was the subject of a long revision process starting in 1989 and finishing in 2003. Enactment of the 2003 amendments by the individual states may start as early as 2004.

The entire Code has undergone revision in the last decade. Article 6 (Bulk Sales) was revised in 1987; Articles 3 (Negotiable Instruments) and 4 (Bank Deposits and Collections) were revised in 1990 with additional amendments in 2002; Article 8 (Investment Securities) was revised in 1994; Article 5 (Letters of Credit) was revised in 1995; Article 9 (Secured Transactions) was completed in 1999; Article 1 (General Provisions) was revised in 2001; and Article 7 (Documents of Title) was completed in 2003. Two new articles, Article 2A (Leases) and Article 4A (Funds Transfers) were added to the Code in 1987 and 1989, respectively. In 2003, amendments to Article 2A (Leases) were adopted to correspond to the amendments to Article 2 and address a few other leasing issues. Because of the ongoing revisions over the last decade, it will be very important for a lawyer to know which version of the Code applies to a particular transaction, as well as to know any nonuniform variation in the statute in the particular state. This text will explore the provisions of Article 2 both prior to and after the 2003 amendments. Some sections of Article 2 were not amended in 2003. If the section was amended, the section will be designated as "revised."

Each article of the Code consists of sections followed by Official Comments. The Official Comments are drafted by the reporter and chair of the drafting committee and explain the text, its operation, and the drafter's intent behind the provisions. The Official Comments are enacted in some states but not in others. In states where they are not enacted, the Official Comments are persuasive authority as to what the text means and how it should be applied, as well as about the interrelationship between different sections. A merchant, for example, is defined in the text of Rev. § 2-104. Official Comment 1 to that section explains the reasons for defining merchants in Article 2. Official Comments 2 and 3 flesh out how the definition should be applied and highlight some of the sections where merchant status matters. In reading any section of the Code, the careful lawyer will also read the Official Comments to gain a better understanding of the meaning and application of the section. Following the Official Comments are cross-references to other Code sections that are relevant to the discussion in the Official Comments, and cross-references to other sections of the Code where relevant terms are defined.

Because Article 2 is only one part of the Code, the provisions of other articles of the Code are often relevant to the analysis of issues. For example, Article 1 contains general provisions, such as definitions, that apply to transactions under Article 2 unless Article 2 has a more specific provision. Provisions from Article 4 and Article 7 on documentary transactions will have relevance in a sale of goods that involves documents of title. Provisions from Article 9 will have relevance when the sale to the buyer is on secured credit. A lawyer seeking to learn how Article 2 applies to a transaction will ignore the other articles of the Code at his or her peril.

The Code also has a relationship to the common law, stated in Rev. § 1-103: "Unless displaced by the particular provisions of [the Uniform Commercial Code], the principles of law and equity" will apply. Revised § 1-103 lists a nonexclusive litany of various common law and equitable areas such as principal and agent, estoppel, fraud and misrepresentation. To understand Article 2, therefore, one must keep in mind common law principles and ask the question whether the particular provision displaces common law and equitable principles or is merely a principle that coexists (sometimes peacefully) with common law and equity.

Finally, one must also keep in mind the admonition of Rev. § 1-103(a) that the provisions of the Act are to be "liberally construed and applied to promote its underlying purposes and policies." Those purposes and policies are as follows:

(a) to simplify, clarify and modernize the law governing commercial transactions;
(b) to permit the continued expansion of commercial practices through custom, usage and agreement of the parties;
(c) to make uniform the law among the various jurisdictions.

B. SCOPE OF ARTICLE 2

Article 2 is entitled "Sales." § 2-101. The Official Comment to § 2-101 states, "the arrangement of the present Article is in terms of contract for sale and the various steps of its performance." The scope provision, § 2-102, however, is arguably broader, providing that Article 2 applies to "transactions in goods." Right at the start, then, is a conflict between the idea of a "contract for sale of goods" and "transactions in goods." "Transaction" is not defined in the Code; whereas, a "sale" is defined as "the passing of title from the seller to the buyer for a price." § 2-106(1). A transaction in goods could be construed to encompass more than just a sale of goods. Until Article 2A was promulgated, for example, a lease of goods could have been a transaction in goods covered under Article 2 even though the transaction was not a sale of goods. Courts relied upon the expansive wording of § 2-102 to justify applying Article 2 to lease transactions. On the other hand, some courts refused to apply Article 2 to a lease transaction because many of the specific substantive provisions of Article 2 are phrased in terms of a "seller" and a "buyer" and are drafted with the paradigm of a sale of goods in mind. Other courts applied selected Article 2 provisions to a lease on a case-by-case basis, relying upon Official Comment 1 to former § 2-105 that invited courts to apply Article 2 by analogy in appropriate cases. This nonuniform approach to leasing existed until Article 2A was promulgated in 1987, thereby making Article 2 inapplicable to a lease transaction. *See* § 2A-102.

This ambiguity concerning the meaning of "transactions in goods" leads to a problem under current law in another respect: whether Article 2 should be applied in a so-called "mixed" transaction. Contracts often involve both the sale of goods and the service or installation of the goods sold. When the transaction is mixed, the courts apply one of two tests: the predominate purpose test (majority view) or the gravamen test (minority view).

Under the predominate purpose test, the court determines whether the predominate purpose of the transaction is to sell the goods or to provide the service. If the predominate purpose is to sell the goods, Article 2 applies. If the predominate purpose is to provide the service, Article 2 does not apply. To determine whether the predominate purpose is to provide the goods or the service, courts generally look at the predominate component in the transaction. To determine what is the predominate component, courts examine many factors including the terminology of the contract, the objective of the parties in entering the contract, the ratio of the price of the goods to the whole price of the contract, the nature of the business of the supplier, and the intrinsic value of the goods without the service.

In contrast, under the gravamen test, the court looks at the basis of the complaint rather than the overall nature of the transaction. If the plaintiff is complaining about the goods component, Article 2 applies. If the plaintiff is complaining about the service component, Article 2 is inapplicable.

- -

EXAMPLE 1: The seller agreed, under a "Material & Equipment" contract with the buyer, to assemble, construct, and install replacement bowling lanes for the buyer's bowling alley and to provide lane-cleaning equipment. Under the contract terms, the buyer ordered and the seller shipped and installed the lanes and equipment. The price included sales tax (which did not apply to services), and the contract warranty extended to the lanes and equipment but not to the installation services. Under the predominate purpose test, the court would look to see whether the primary purpose of this contract was to provide the goods; if so, Article 2 would apply. If the predominate purpose was to supply a service, non–Article 2 contract law would apply. The dominant aspect of this contract appears to be provision of the goods with the installation being incidental because of the terminology used in the contract, the parties' objectives in entering the contract, and the nature of the supplier's services. Under the gravamen test, the court would look at whether the complaint was with the goods or with the installation service. If the problem was with the parts of the lane or the pinsetting equipment, Article 2 would apply. If the problem was with how the lanes or equipment were installed, then Article 2 would not apply.

Article 2 only applies to transactions involving goods. The definition of the term "goods" prior to the 2003 amendments was "all things . . . which are movable at the time of identification to the contract for sale other than the money in which the price is to be paid, investment securities (Article 8) and things in action. 'Goods' also includes the unborn young of animals and growing crops and other identified things attached to realty as described in the section on goods to be severed from realty (Section 2-107)." Former § 2-105(1). This language raised the question of what it meant to have a "movable thing," the linchpin of the definition of "good." An example is the courts' struggle over whether sale of electricity is a sale of a "good." The court cases on this issue are mixed. Labor, services, and investment securities (such as bonds and stocks) are not considered "goods." A cause of action is not a "good."

The 2003 amendments to Article 2 revised the definition of "goods" in Rev. § 2-103(1)(k) to exclude "information" and "the subject matter of foreign exchange transactions" in addition to the exclusions from the definition of goods in former § 2-105. Thus, Article 2 does not apply directly to a transaction that consists only of providing information, unconnected to any goods.

The term "information" is not defined but is intended to cover at least computer programs. If a transaction involves both information and goods, however, the courts will have to resolve whether to apply Article 2 in whole or in part to the transaction. Whether the courts will use some version of the predominate purpose test or the gravamen test or another standard yet to be created for making that determination remains to be seen. A "foreign exchange transaction" is defined in Rev. § 2-103(1)(i) as an agreement for trading in foreign currencies where the settlement takes place through debiting or crediting account balances. If the settlement takes place through physical delivery of specie or money, however, the transaction is not a foreign exchange transaction and would be covered by Article 2.

Section 2-107 provides that minerals, oil, gas, and buildings to be severed from the realty are goods if the seller severs them. If the buyer is to sever the oil and gas, then the contract for sale would not be governed by Article 2. The possible sources of law for this type of transaction are common law contract rights for services of extraction or perhaps real estate law if the transaction is to transfer property rights. If a contract for sale is made after severance of such items as oil and gas, those items are "goods." On the other hand, growing crops or timber or other things that can be severed without material harm to the land are goods even before severance without regard to who will sever those items.

The final clause of § 2-102 states that Article 2 does not apply to a transaction that is intended to operate as a security transaction. A security transaction is governed by Article 9. Assume that a buyer wants to purchase goods but the buyer does not want to pay for the goods at sale. The parties agree to a conditional sales contract in which the seller retains title to the goods until full payment of the price. This is both a sale and a secured transaction, and Article 9 would apply. The Official Comment to § 2-102 states that Article 2 governs the sale aspects of the transaction, such as warranty or delivery terms, as between the buyer and seller. Article 9 would govern the security arrangement aspects, such as priority among third parties.

The final clause of § 2-102 states that Article 2 does not repeal or impair statutes enacted for particular classes of buyers, such as consumers or farmers. This clause is included to ensure that state statutes that provide special protections for certain types of people are still in force and effect even after Article 2 is enacted. This is necessary to prevent a statutory interpretation argument that the later-enacted statute overrides the earlier-enacted statute—or the statutory interpretation canon that a more specific statute overrides a more general statute. Examples of state consumer protection statutes include the Uniform Consumer Credit Code, a retail installment sales act, or a "plain English" statute that mandates a certain type of language in consumer contracts.

Amended Article 2 contains a new section, Rev. § 2-108, which makes clear that if a transaction subject to Article 2 also is subject to another type of law specified in this section, in the event of a conflict, the other law controls, with one exception. The other law referred to in this section is of three types: (1) certificate of title laws, (2) consumer law, and (3) statutes dealing with particular types of products or transactions, such as agricultural products, human blood and tissue, consignments of art by artists, distribution or franchise agreements, food and drug misbranding or adulteration, and regulation of product dealers. The one exception to the deference to other law is that the Article 2 rule on entrustment stated in Rev. § 2-403(2), protecting a buyer in ordinary course, will prevail over a contrary rule in a certificate of title statute in one situation. If a buyer in ordinary course has rights that arise before a certificate of title is issued in the name of any other buyer, the Article 2 entrustment rule will prevail over a contrary rule in a certificate of title law. Rev. § 2-108 also provides that the rules in Article 2 will supercede the provisions of the federal Electronic Signatures in Global and National Commerce Act ("E-Sign") except for certain types of consumer notices described in 15 U.S.C. § 7001(c) and notices exempted from E-Sign in 15 U.S.C. § 7003(c). Thus, to the extent that Article 2 has rules that support electronic commerce, those rules will take precedence over the rules stated in E-Sign with the noted exceptions.

C. CONCEPT OF CONTRACT

The vehicle for a sale of goods is a contract between the buyer and the seller. In Article 2, the words "contract" or "agreement" are limited to those contracts or agreements "relating to the present or future sale of goods." § 2-106(1). The Code distinguishes between an agreement and a contract. An "agreement" is the "bargain of the parties in fact." Rev. § 1-201(b)(3). The "contract" is "the total legal obligation that results from the parties' agreement as determined by [the Uniform Commercial Code] as supplemented by any other applicable laws." Rev. § 1-201(b)(12). Article 2's concept of agreement and hence of contract is much broader than what the common law of contracts might consider to be a contract. The parties' bargain in fact may be determined from the parties' language or be implied from the parties' course of dealing, usage of trade, or the course of performance. Rev. § 1-201(b)(3); Rev. § 1-303.

These three phrases mean that the parties' own behavior and the practices of an industry will fill in the "gaps" left when the parties expressly have agreed on only a few major points. The parties need not agree explicitly on every term. Article 2 principles and the parties' behavior and industry practice will fill in terms where the parties have not explicitly agreed and become part of the parties' bargain in fact. Rev. § 1-201(b)(3). Finally, the parties' behavior and industry practice will serve as interpretive guides of what the parties meant by the terms to which they have expressly agreed. This realistic approach to contract formation and terms will be explained in succeeding chapters.

Even though Article 2 contains basic principles to be applied in the sale of goods contract, it is not primarily designed as a regulation of the parties' agreement. Unless a section provides that it may not be varied by agreement, each principle in Article 2 can be varied by agreement with the exception of the obligations of "good faith, diligence, reasonableness, and care prescribed by [the Uniform Commercial Code]." Rev. § 1-302(a). Thus, Article 2 is based upon the principle of freedom to contract. Rev. § 1-302,

Official Comment 1. Freedom of contract means that with very few exceptions, the parties are free to agree and free not to agree to particular terms in a sale of goods contract. Freedom of contract has its down side in that it can lead to overreaching or what observers of particular transactions might say is an unfair deal between parties of unequal power. Be that as it may, the Article 2 drafters opted not to provide for a minimum fair deal in a sale of goods transaction, relying instead on the protective legislation referred to in § 2-102 and Rev. § 2-108 to protect parties perceived to be unable to protect themselves.

D. CONSUMER V. COMMERCIAL TRANSACTIONS

Article 2 applies to all sales of goods whether conducted by a business or an individual. Thus, if I sell you a pencil, Article 2 applies. If you buy one pencil or a gross of pencils from the local office supply store, Article 2 applies. If a major corporation purchases twenty tons of steel from another major corporation, Article 2 applies. Article 2 applies regardless of whether the buyer or the seller is a consumer or a merchant.

EXAMPLE 2: Tired of owning an old car, the seller sold the car to his next-door neighbor. Article 2 applies to the transaction.

EXAMPLE 3: The buyer bought a car from B's Used Car Sales. Article 2 applies to the transaction.

EXAMPLE 4: MegaCorp, Inc., an interstate trucking company, bought a fleet of new trucks from MotorTrucks, Inc. Article 2 applies to this transaction.

As stated above, Article 2 does not override any other state law regarding consumers. Article 2 supplements any consumer protection statute. In the case of a conflict, the consumer protection statute will control. § 2-102; Rev. § 2-108.

EXAMPLE 5: In Example 3 above, if the state had enacted a consumer protection statute for car sales, both Article 2 and the consumer protection statute would apply to the transaction.

Article 2 does have some specific provisions dealing with contracts with merchants or between merchants. A transaction is between merchants if both parties are chargeable with the knowledge or skills of a merchant. Rev. § 2-104(3). A merchant is a person who (1) deals in goods of the kind sold, (2) by the person's occupation holds itself out as having knowledge or skills peculiar to the practices or goods involved in the transaction, or (3) employs an agent, broker, or other intermediary who by occupation holds itself out as having knowledge or skills peculiar to the practices or goods involved in the transaction. Rev. § 2-104(1). As Official Comments 2 and 3 of § 2-104 point out, whether a party is a merchant in a particular transaction depends upon the facts of the case. A party may be a merchant either because of dealing in goods of that kind or because of the party's knowledge and skill. The applicability of certain provisions of Article 2 depends upon what type of merchant the party is in that transaction. For example, the warranty of merchantability is given only by merchants who deal in goods of that kind but not by parties who are merchants because of their occupation and skills. Rev. § 2-314.

Prior to the 2003 amendments, good faith for non-merchants was limited to "honesty in fact" and for merchants included as well "reasonable commercial standards of fair dealing in the trade." Former § 2-103(1)(b). The 2003 amendments to Article 2 changed the general obligation of good faith by defining "good faith" for merchants and non-merchants alike to include not only "honesty in fact" but also "reasonable commercial standards of fair dealing." Rev. § 2-103(1)(j).

EXAMPLE 6: In Example 4 (trucking company buying trucks from truck dealership), both parties were merchants with respect to those goods, so the provisions of Article 2 governing transactions "between merchants" would apply in addition to the other provisions of Article 2. In Example 2 (consumer selling car to neighbor), Article 2 provisions concerning merchants would not apply but the rest of Article 2 would apply. In Example 3 (consumer buying car from used car lot), Article 2 provisions that govern when the seller was a merchant would apply as well as all of the other provisions of Article 2.

- -

Even though a particular provision might apply when one party is a merchant or when both parties are merchants, the basic thrust of Article 2 is to apply its provisions to a transaction even if neither party is a merchant.

CHAPTER

TWO

CONTRACT FORMATION: THE SIMPLE CASE

A. FORMATION IN GENERAL

The basic requirements for contract formation under Article 2 do not vary greatly from the common law. Article 2 also has, over the years, influenced common law contract principles so that common law principles and Article 2 principles have become even more similar. As stated previously, Article 2 incorporates, in supplementary fashion, the entire common law of contracts into its provisions, except where the common law is "displaced by the particular provisions of the [Uniform Commercial Code]." Rev. § 1-103. As a result, common law legal and equitable principles must be kept in mind when analyzing the Article 2 requirements for contracts. Article 2 does not attempt to restate all of the rules of contract formation; the contract formation rules stated in Article 2 can be viewed as legislation against technical and formalized common law rules that the Article 2 drafters thought impaired courts' ability to enforce the parties' actual agreement.

In any contract, there are always two issues: first, whether a contract has been formed, and second, what are the terms of that contract. The provisions on contract formation will be discussed in this chapter and the provisions on contract terms will be discussed in Chapters 3 and 4. These three chapters focus on contract formation and terms in the simple case. Chapter 5 discusses contract formation and terms in the more difficult case, the battle of the forms situation.

The provisions on contact formation in Article 2 center on the parties' agreement with the basic formation rule in Rev. § 2-204(1): "[a] contract for sale of goods may be made in any manner sufficient to show agreement." As the 2003 amendments make clear, agreement can be shown by conduct, by an offer and acceptance, by the use of electronic agents, or by any other credible evidence of an intent to be bound. Thus, while Article 2 recognizes traditional modes of contract formation, it is much more liberal in its approach and was designed to change the heavy reliance on the technical rules of offer and acceptance in order to find a contract.

EXAMPLE 1: A retailer and a manufacturer discussed a possible sale of stereos over the telephone. The next day, the manufacturer shipped the stereos. When the retailer received the stereos, it displayed those stereos in the store for sale. The retailer sold some of the stereos to customers. Even though the discussion between the retailer and the manufacturer, standing alone, might not have constituted a contract for sale, the parties' conduct in shipping and accepting the goods was enough to indicate an agreement.

In this example, a contract could have been formed during the discussion or by the subsequent conduct. Isolation of the offer and the acceptance is not required. Revised § 2-204(2) provides that it does not matter if the moment of making the contract cannot be pinned down; a contract still has been formed.

Under Article 2 even though the parties have not agreed on all of the terms of the agreement, a contract still may be formed, eliminating another common law formation rule that required the parties to agree to all of the material terms before a contract was formed. Revised § 2-204(3) provides that a contract is not too indefinite to be formed merely because the parties did not agree on every term. All that is required is sufficient evidence that the parties intended to contract and that there is a reasonably certain basis for giving a remedy. The number and importance of omitted terms will be relevant to determining whether the parties intended to contract but will not necessarily preclude the finding that a contract was formed. Thus, Rev. § 2-204 broadens the enforceability of contract by focusing on the parties' agreement, the bargain in fact, and displaces the common law rules that accord importance to ascertaining the time of formation and the definiteness of all of the terms.

B. ELECTRONIC CONTRACTING

The 2003 amendments to § 2-204 make clear that if an electronic agent is used, a contract may be formed through the action of the electronic agent. An electronic agent is a computer program or automated means used to initiate or respond to electronic input without an individual reviewing the action. Rev. § 2-103(1)(g). These provisions regarding formation of a contract through use of an electronic agent are derived from the Uniform Electronic Transactions Act and are "intended to negate any claim that lack of human intent, at the time of contract formation, prevents contract formation." Rev. § 2-204, Official Comment 4.

Other provisions added by the 2003 amendments also support the use of electronics in contract formation. Throughout amended Article 2, the word "record" has been substituted for the word "writing." A "record" is "information that is inscribed on a tangible medium or that is stored in an electronic or other medium and is retrievable in perceivable form." Rev. § 2-103(1)(m). The word "signed" has also been revised to accommodate electronic signatures. Rev. § 2-103(1)(p). New definitions of "electronic," "electronic agent," and "electronic record" have been added. Rev. § 2-103(1)(f) through (h). To support electronic contracting, new rules have been added providing:

- A signature or record may not be denied effect just because it is in electronic form. Rev. § 2-211(1).
- A contract may not be denied effect just because electronic records were used in its formation. Rev. § 2-211(2).
- An electronic record or signature is attributable to a person if it was that person's act, its electronic agent's act, or otherwise attributable to that person under other law. Rev. § 2-212.
- Electronic communications may have legal effect even if no individual is aware of the receipt. Rev. § 2-213(1).
- Receipt of an electronic communication does not establish that the content sent corresponds to the content received. Rev. § 2-213(2).
- If a contract is formed through the use of an electronic agent, the contract terms do not include terms provided by an individual if the individual had reason to know that the electronic agent could not react to the terms. Rev. § 2-211(4).

Although the 2003 amendments to Article 2 support the use of electronics in contract formation, nothing in Article 2 requires electronics be used. Rev. § 2-211(3). These rules are designed to make Article 2 medium neutral and dispel objections that may be made concerning the use of electronics in contract formation.

C. FORMATION BY OFFER AND ACCEPTANCE

Article 2 follows the common law in contract formation through offer and acceptance. Article 2 does not change the common law rules of an offer. An offer is a manifestation of an intent to make a contract, where that manifestation could be construed reasonably under the circumstances as inviting acceptance. Just as with the common law contract formation rules, Article 2 allows the offeror to specify the permissible manners of acceptance by the offeree. Rev. § 2-206(1).

Article 2 does, however, change some of the common law rules of offer and acceptance. For example, if the offeror does not specify a required means of acceptance, the offer "shall be construed as inviting acceptance in any manner and by any medium reasonable in the circumstances." Rev. § 2-206(1)(a). At common law, the acceptance is not effective when sent unless the acceptance is communicated in a manner invited by the offeror. For example, courts presumed that an offer sent by mail invites acceptance by mail. In that circumstance, the acceptance is effective upon mailing. If the acceptance was not made in the same manner as the offer, however, then the court's presumption that the acceptance is effective when sent would not necessarily apply. In Article 2, the acceptance need not be communicated in the same medium as the offer as long as the communication of acceptance is reasonable under the circumstances, unless the offeror specifies to the contrary. The focus of what medium of acceptance is reasonable under the circumstances continues Article 2's focus on the real context of the parties' commercial situation rather than on technical legal rules that might not work in practice.

EXAMPLE 2: The manufacturer sent a written offer to the retailer for the sale of 300 stereos at $100 per stereo. The offer stated merely that the retailer should "let the manufacturer know" whether the retailer accepted the offer. The retailer telephoned the next day and told the manufacturer that he accepted the offer and the manufacturer recorded the subject of the call in his daily log. In this situation, the retailer accepted the offer and contract formation occurred. A telephone call in response to a written offer is reasonable in this circumstance. If the manufacturer's written offer had provided that the retailer should "sign and return the enclosed counterpart of the letter signaling your acceptance," the manufacturer would have specified the medium of acceptance. In order to have an acceptance, the retailer would have to act as instructed to accept the offer.

Consistent with these rules, an offeror can request acceptance by either a return promise (bilateral contract) or a performance of the contract (unilateral contract). When it is unclear which type of acceptance the offeror has requested, either will suffice. Rev. § 2-206(1)(a). This changes the pre-Code common law result in some cases. Under the common law, there was a legal presumption that an offer required acceptance by return promise if the actual offer was ambiguous about the requisite form of acceptance.

Where an order or other offer is made to buy goods that will be shipped under the contract, either shipment of the goods or a prompt promise to ship the goods is a proper means of acceptance, unless otherwise specified by the offeror. Rev. § 2-206(1)(b). Thus, a seller who receives a purchase order for goods may simply ship conforming goods, and the shipment will constitute acceptance of the offer. Revised § 2-206(1)(b) also addresses the situation where the seller responds to the order by shipping nonconforming goods. Under the common law, the seller's shipment of goods that do not conform to the offer is a counteroffer. If the buyer accepts the goods, there is a contract on the terms of the counteroffer. If the buyer rejects the goods, there is no contract. Revised § 2-206(1)(b) changes this result. If the seller informs the buyer that the goods shipped are nonconforming and offered only as an accommodation to the buyer, then the shipment does not constitute an acceptance of the buyer's offer. *Id.* The shipment by the seller constitutes a counteroffer that the buyer may accept, thereby forming a contract, or reject, resulting in no contract. *Id.* However, if the seller does not state that the shipment is merely an accommodation, the shipment is simultaneously acceptance of the original offer and a breach of the resulting contract.

EXAMPLE 3: The retailer offered to buy 400 Model Z stereos from the manufacturer for $40,000. The manufacturer shipped 400 Model Y stereos with a memo that stated: "Cannot ship Model Z, out of stock. Model Y is offered hoping it satisfies your needs." In that situation, the shipment does not constitute acceptance but is a counteroffer. At that point in time, no contract existed. The manufacturer has not accepted the retailer's offer to buy and the retailer has not accepted the manufacturer's counteroffer to sell.

EXAMPLE 4: In the same situation as Example 3, the manufacturer's memo sent with the Model Y stereos stated: "Hope these will satisfy you." That memo does not state that the nonconforming goods were offered as an accommodation to the buyer. The delivery of the Model Y stereos constituted acceptance of the retailer's offer to buy and a contract was formed. In addition, if Model Y and Model Z stereos were different, then the manufacturer has both accepted the offer and breached the contract in shipping the goods.

Article 2 also addresses the troublesome issue of offer revocation in Rev. § 2-206(2), which restricts an offeror's ability to revoke an offer "if the beginning of a requested performance is a reasonable mode of acceptance . . . ." Commencement of the requested performance by the offeree is an acceptance of the offer as long as the offeree gives notice of acceptance to the offeror within a "reasonable time." Rev. § 2-206(2). This notice to the offeree is to protect the offeree and the offeror. The offeror needs protection from having unknowingly formed a contract when the offeree begins performance. The offeror might not know that the offeree has accepted and may contract with someone else. The offeree needs protection from the offeror revoking the offer and the offeree in the meantime having incurred costs in starting to perform. If the offeree does not provide notice of acceptance within a reasonable time, the offeror can treat the offer as having lapsed before acceptance. Rev. § 2-206(2). This situation often arises in the case of specially manufactured goods.

EXAMPLE 5: The retailer sent an offer to buy ten specially built stereos from the manufacturer. The manufacturer received the offer and started to build the stereos the next day. Later that week, approximately five days after receiving the retailer's offer, the manufacturer called the retailer to tell the retailer it had started performance. The retailer in the meantime had contracted with a distributor to procure the ten specially built stereos. The retailer only needed one set of ten specially built stereos. If the manufacturer's start on building the stereos was a reasonable mode of acceptance, a contract was formed with the retailer at that time. The retailer, however, may treat its offer to buy as lapsed if the time that elapsed between when the manufacturer received and accepted the offer and the notice of the acceptance to the retailer was more than a reasonable time. In that case, no contract with the manufacturer would have been formed.

D. FIRM OFFERS

Under the common law, an offeror generally is not placed under a contractual obligation until his offer is accepted, and usually an offer is freely revokable until it is accepted by the offeree. The offeree may, however, request that the offeror keep the offer open for a specified period of time. Under Article 2, this type of irrevocable offer is called a "firm offer." Article 2 does not require the offeree to give additional consideration to make a firm offer enforceable. This is a change from the common law under which an offer is considered irrevocable only if consideration is given in exchange for the promise to keep the offer open. In the absence of consideration, under the common law the offer is freely revokable even if the agreement provided specifically that the offer was irrevocable.

Revised § 2-205, as updated by the 2003 amendments, provides that for the sale of goods, a firm offer is irrevocable if (i) there is an actual offer, (ii) the offer is made by a merchant, and (iii) the offer is given in a signed record providing assurances that it will be held open. The record requirement substitutes for consideration in this context. Though it is not always clear what constitutes sufficient "assurances" that the offer will remain open, statements such as "offer to remain open for thirty days" usually suffice. Merely stating that an offer will expire in thirty days might not be sufficient assurance, however, that the offer cannot be revoked before the end of the thirty-day time period. If an offer is made in accordance with the noted requirements, the offer will remain irrevocable for the specified period of time.

Furthermore, if no time period is specified, then the offer will remain irrevocable for a "reasonable time." In either circumstance, the period of irrevocability cannot exceed three months. Rev. § 2-205. Revised § 2-205 also provides additional protection to the offeror by providing that if the statement of the firm offer is in a form supplied by the offeree, the statement must be signed separately by the offeror for the offer to be a firm offer.

E. STATUTE OF FRAUDS

1. IN GENERAL

Although parties may form an agreement under Article 2 without any written evidence, sometimes the lack of a writing may prevent the agreement from being enforced as the legal obligation of the parties. This bar to enforceability without a writing was stated in former § 2-201. The 2003 amendments update the statute by replacing the word "writing" with the word "record." The purpose of the record requirement is to prevent fraud in the presentation of evidence to a trier of fact of an alleged deal that is completely oral. The theory is that a record provides objective evidence that a contract might exist. The statute of frauds has been subject to extensive criticism because it allows fraud of a different sort, such as a party claiming that no record exists in order to avoid living up to a bargain that was actually made.

To understand the operation of Rev. § 2-201, one must clearly separate the statute of frauds record requirement from the issue of contract formation. Having a record that satisfies Rev. § 2-201 does not prove a contract exists nor does it prove the terms of the contract. All the record does is to allow the party who alleges a contract was made to present evidence of that fact to a trier of fact. Even if a record that satisfies Rev. § 2-201 exists, a trier of fact can legitimately find, as a matter of fact, that no contract was made under the rules of contract formation discussed above. This role of the statute of frauds is borne out in Official Comment 1 to Rev. § 2-201, which states, "[a]ll that is required is that the record afford a reasonable basis to determine that the offered oral evidence rests on a real transaction." A party who gets past the hurdle of Rev. § 2-201 must still prove both the existence of the contract and its enforceable terms.

2. BASIC APPLICATION OF THE STATUTE OF FRAUDS

Revised § 2-201(1) provides that a contract for the sale of goods when the price is $5,000 or more (changed from $500 or more under former Article 2) is not enforceable unless a record exists that is sufficient to indicate a contract has been made and is signed by the party against whom enforcement is sought or that party's agent. The record need not state all of the terms and need not state terms accurately. If such a record exists and a contract is found, then the contract is not enforceable beyond the quantity term stated in the record. This record need not be in any special form, nor must it be signed contemporaneously with contract formation.

EXAMPLE 6: The manufacturer's authorized salesperson met with the retailer in a local bar. The salesperson offered to sell 100 computers to the retailer at $1,000 apiece. The retailer orally accepted the offer. The salesperson and the retailer then had a couple of drinks and shot several games of pool. Before they left for the evening, the retailer wrote on the back of his business card, "100 computers, $1,000 per" and gave it to the salesperson. Two days later the 100 computers arrived on the retailer's loading dock. The retailer refused to accept the computers, claiming that no contract existed. The business card is a record and states the quantity term. The issue is whether the retailer "signed" the record. If the retailer adopted the information on the face of the business card with the present intent to authenticate the record, the record is signed and the business card satisfies the statute of frauds. The manufacturer will still have to prove that a contract existed and the terms of that contract. The business card is one piece of evidence but not conclusive on those issues.

EXAMPLE 7: The retailer called the manufacturer and offered to buy 100 computers for $1,000 per computer, delivery in one week. The manufacturer replied to the phone call by sending an e-mail accepting the offer but mistyped the quantity term as 10 computers. The manufacturer's e-mail had a signature file appended to the message which stated the manufacturer's name, address, phone and fax numbers, and e-mail address. When only 10 computers arrived from the manufacturer, the retailer sued for breach of contract because of the non-delivery of 90 computers. The e-mail will satisfy the statute of frauds. The contract is not enforceable beyond the quantity of 10 computers stated in the E-mail.

Several records, as well as a single record, may perform the evidentiary function of indicating that a contract may have been formed, if at least one of the records has been signed by the party against whom enforcement is sought and the several records relate to the same transaction.

3. MERCHANT CONFIRMATIONS

Revised § 2-201(2) provides the one exception to the requirement that there be a signature by the party against whom enforcement is sought. Where both parties are merchants, one party cannot invoke Rev. § 2-201 to bar enforcement of an alleged contract when a record in confirmation of the contract is received by that party within a reasonable time and that party failed to object to the contents of the confirmation within ten days of its receipt. Rev. § 2-201(2). The confirmation has to satisfy the requirements discussed above (record, signed, and stating a quantity term) against the party who sent the confirmation and the party receiving the confirmation has to have reason to know of its contents. Not every record that sets out the terms of the agreement is a "confirmation." A confirmation requires the existence of a previous agreement. Therefore, the parties must have already formed a contract for the record to be a confirmation of the contract.

- -

> EXAMPLE 8: The retailer orally offered to buy 100 computers at $1,000 per computer from the manufacturer for sale in the retailer's store. The manufacturer accepted the offer orally. The next day, the manufacturer sent a letter to the retailer that stated: "Pursuant to our conversation yesterday, 100 computers, $1,000 per unit have been shipped today." The manufacturer signed the letter. The retailer received the letter and did not respond. When the computers arrived on the retailer's loading dock, the retailer refused to accept the computers, claiming no contract with the manufacturer. Both parties are merchants in this transaction. Even though the retailer had not signed a record, the confirmation that the manufacturer sent is sufficient to satisfy the statute of frauds under Rev. § 2-201(2) because the retailer failed to object to that confirmation. The retailer is barred from raising the statute of frauds defense.

- -

4. EXCEPTIONS TO THE RECORD REQUIREMENT

Revised § 2-201(3) contains three exceptions to the requirement that there be a record as provided in Rev. § 2-201(1). In those three situations, the absence of a record will not bar a party moving forward with evidence to prove the existence and terms of a contract. In addition, nonstatutory exceptions to the record requirement imposed in Rev. § 2-201(1) also exist.

The first exception, Rev. § 2-201(3)(a), negates the need for a record when the seller acts reasonably in reliance on an oral contract for specially manufactured goods, where the goods are not marketable to others in the ordinary course of the seller's business. Under this exception to the record requirement, the seller must have either begun substantially to manufacture the goods or received commitments for their procurement before the receipt of notice of the buyer's repudiation. The reason for this exception is that the commencement of manufacturing or procurement, in the case of goods that cannot be sold to anyone else, provides objective evidence that the parties have an agreement.

EXAMPLE **9:** A car dealer orally ordered 300 logo decals of the dealer's name for placement on the back of new cars the dealer holds for sale. The manufacturer orally accepted the order and began to manufacture the decals. The next day, the dealer changed its mind and called to cancel the order. The manufacturer could seek to enforce the contract against the retailer even though no record exists because the decals would not be marketable to anyone else.

The second exception to the record requirement, Rev. § 2-201(3)(b), is that no record is needed when the party seeking to bar enforcement of the contract admits in pleadings, testimony, or otherwise under oath that a contract exists. The 2003 amendments changed the former language from admissions "in court" to "under oath" in recognition of the reality of the litigation process. The contract is enforceable against the party making the admission to the extent of the quantity admitted. These admissions provide objective evidence of the existence of a contract.

EXAMPLE **10:** The retailer filed a complaint alleging an oral deal with the manufacturer. The manufacturer moved for summary judgment on the ground that no record satisfying Rev. § 2-201 existed. At the deposition of the manufacturer's salesperson, the salesperson stated, "Yeah, we agreed to ship 100 computers, but we didn't write it down so it doesn't count." A deposition is "under oath." The salesperson's statement is an admission of an agreement and the statute of frauds defense should fail. The agreement should be enforceable to the extent of 100 computers.

Unfortunately the example just given is somewhat unrealistic. The usual scenario is that the plaintiff alleges in the complaint an oral contract. The defendant brings a motion to dismiss asserting that the complaint does not allege a record sufficient to satisfy the statute of frauds. In most jurisdictions, the defendant bringing a motion to dismiss does not admit the truth of the alleged case as stated in the complaint. At the motion to dismiss stage, the absence of an allegation in the complaint of a record may result in the dismissal of the complaint even if a contract existed, although some jurisdictions will not entertain a motion to dismiss until there has been a chance for discovery on the issue of whether a contract existed. Dismissing an action for breach of contract when a contract, but not a record, exists is the source of much criticism of the statute of frauds. Another criticism of this exception is the tendency of the exception to encourage perjury. Because a party cannot admit the existence of a contract and still assert a defense, if the proceeding advances to the discovery stage, a defendant may wrongly deny that a contract exists to preserve the statute of frauds defense.

The third exception to the record requirement, Rev. § 2-201(3)(c), is that a record is not required when payment has been made and accepted or the goods have been received and accepted to the extent of the payment or the amount of goods accepted. Accepting the goods or accepting payment for goods is again a good objective indication that an agreement exists.

EXAMPLE 11: The retailer and the manufacturer orally agreed that the manufacturer will ship 100 sets of Model 213 speakers at $100 per set. The retailer sent a certified check for $5,000 to the manufacturer. The manufacturer deposited the check in its bank account but did not ship the speakers. The retailer can enforce the contract, but for only 50 sets of speakers. That was the quantity for which the retailer paid and the manufacturer accepted payment.

EXAMPLE 12: The retailer and the manufacturer orally agreed that the manufacturer would ship 100 sets of Model 213 speakers at $100 per set. The manufacturer shipped 50 sets, and the retailer accepted them. The manufacturer shipped the rest of the sets and the retailer returned them to the manufacturer. The manufacturer can enforce the contract but only as to the 50 sets that the retailer accepted.

- -

Prior to the 2003 amendments to Article 2, some courts recognized nonstatutory exceptions to the requirements of former § 2-201. These exceptions were based upon estoppel and fraud. Those courts that did so generally relied on former § 1-103 and held that former § 2-201 did not explicitly displace equitable estoppel and fraud principles. The courts that did not recognize these exceptions contended that former § 2-201 explicitly displaced these equitable principles. The concern with the estoppel and fraud exceptions to the requirement of § 2-201 is that these exceptions, if applied in full force, might swallow the rule, completely excusing a record requirement in a large percentage of cases where the courts find that an oral agreement has been made. In the 2003 amendments, the language at the beginning of former § 2-201(1), "except as otherwise provided in this section," was deleted. The new Official Comment 2 to Rev. § 2-201 states that this was done to allow estoppel principles to provide an exception to the record requirement.

Estoppel that prevents assertion of the record requirement can be found if there is reasonable detrimental reliance on conduct or promises. For example, a court might find that a promise was made or that one party acted in such a way as to lead the other party to think a deal was made, that the other party reasonably relied on the promise or conduct, and that the relying party was injured. The party who relied is the one alleging a contract. Finding that the elements of estoppel exist, the court will excuse the record requirement and allow the party alleging the deal to go ahead and submit evidence regarding the existence of the agreement and its terms. These facts may not be unusual in many cases. What promise or conduct can be relied upon to estop a party from asserting the record requirement will vary in the cases. Some courts have found that the promise must relate to whether a record is necessary. Other courts have found that the promise merely can be the promised performance under the alleged contract.

The fraud exception is based upon the courts' finding that one cannot use the record requirement to perpetrate a fraud. In cases that cite the fraud exception, the courts reason that if an oral agreement were actually made, asserting a record requirement as a bar to the enforcement of that agreement would be fraudulent. Applied with full force, this reasoning greatly undermines the reason for a record requirement in the first instance.

The 2003 amendments also added a new subsection to Rev. § 2-201 providing that if a contract satisfies the Article 2 statute of frauds, other statutes of frauds should not be used to bar enforceability of the contract. Rev. § 2-201(4). That amendment along with the deletion of former § 1-106 from Article 1 means that if a contract within Article 2 satisfies the statute of frauds in Rev. § 2-201, including being under the dollar amount necessary for the statute to apply, the contract should not be unenforceable based upon a statute of frauds other than Rev. § 2-201.

CHAPTER

THREE

CONTRACT TERMS:
THE SIMPLE CASE

Once a contract is formed, the next question is what are the terms of the contract. In responding to this question, Article 2 has three categories of rules. First, as discussed in Chapter 2, the parties need not expressly agree on every term to have an enforceable contract. Article 2 contains many provisions that constitute implied terms in the contract and help to fill in the "gaps" in the parties' express agreement. These terms are referred to as "default terms." Second, terms in a contract may need to be interpreted because language can be susceptible to several interpretations. To the extent not displaced by particular provisions of Article 2, the common law rules for contract interpretation will apply to the terms of a contract formed under Article 2. Finally, the parties will sometimes memorialize their agreement in a record. When they do so, the issue arises of whether terms allegedly agreed to by the parties, but not in the record, are to be considered part of the agreement. Article 2 contains a parol evidence rule to address this situation.

A. EXPRESS, IMPLIED, AND DEFAULT TERMS

The Code defines an agreement as the parties' "bargain in fact." This bargain is based upon terms to which the parties have expressly agreed by their language. In addition, terms may be implied as part of the "bargain in fact" by the parties' course of performance, course of dealing, and usage of trade. Rev. § 1-201(b)(3).

1. EXPRESS TERMS

Express terms of an agreement include whatever the parties have agreed to in record or in verbal or other communication. For example, express terms may be found in the offer, the acceptance, brochures, labels, or any other type of medium.

Article 2 generally embraces the concept of freedom of contract. Except as provided in Rev. § 1-302, parties are free to define the terms of their agreement. The parties may not disclaim the "obligations of good faith, diligence, reasonableness and care prescribed" by the Code. Rev. § 1-302. The contracting parties may set the standards for performance of those duties as long as the standards are not manifestly unreasonable. Rev. § 1-302(b). "Good faith" means "honesty in fact and the observance of reasonable commercial standards of fair dealing." Rev. § 2-103(1)(j). As stated in Chapter 1, this standard of good faith will apply to all transactions covered by amended Article 2, not just to transactions involving merchants.

Most of the Code provisions may be varied by agreement or waived unless a variance or a waiver is prohibited. Rev. § 1-302(a). The prohibition of variance or waiver may be either express or implied. For example, though neither Rev. § 2-201 nor its Official Comments state that the statute of frauds record requirement cannot be waived orally, Official Comment 1 to Rev. § 1-302 provides that a fair reading of both former and Rev. § 2-201 indicates that such an oral waiver would defeat the requirement for a writing/record. Similarly, the Code does not state specifically that the bar against unconscionable provisions cannot be waived. Nonetheless, courts have held consistently that the requirements of former § 2-302 (barring enforcement of unconscionable provisions) and § 2-719(3) (providing that an exclusion of personal injury damages in the case of consumer goods is unconscionable) may not be waived or altered by agreement between the parties. To hold otherwise would go against the substantive policy of those sections, which protect against unfair behavior in the contracting process. Finally, the rights of third parties under Rev. § 2-403 may not be waived or altered by agreement between the contracting parties. This is logical inasmuch as the third party is not a party to the agreement and, therefore, should not be bound by it.

The provisions of Article 2 usually can be displaced expressly by simple language. A few provisions, such as Rev. § 2-316, which sets out the procedures for disclaiming or modifying warranties, only can be altered or displaced by specific language or in a specific manner. Also, some Article 2 sections, such as Rev. § 2-209, which sets out the procedure for creating an enforceable "no-oral-modification clause," establish the manner in which certain terms may be agreed upon.

2. IMPLIED TERMS

Course of Performance.   Contract terms can be implied through the parties' course of performance. Where a party to a contract knows of, and has a chance to object to, the other party's conduct during performance of a contract, the nature of that conduct becomes relevant in determining the meaning of the contract. Rev. § 1-303(a). The underlying theory in allowing the parties' course of performance to become part of the agreement is that a repeated course of action by one party and acquiescence by the other suggests the existence of an agreement to that mode of performance.

Course of performance refers only to the parties' performance of the contract in issue and not to either parties' actions under prior contracts. Consequently, only a party's actions subsequent to the formation of the instant contract and in performance of that contract can be considered in determining the parties' course of performance. Rev. § 1-303, Official Comment 2. A party's actions will not be considered course of performance, admissible to interpret or supply terms to the contract, unless the other contracting party had knowledge of the actions and acquiesced to them without objection. Rev. § 1-303(a).

- -

> EXAMPLE 1: A processor in Iowa contracted to sell to a feed supply in Idaho twenty installments of processed rice. The parties did not specifically agree on who should pay the freight. For each of the first ten deliveries, the processor instructed the carrier to bill the feed supply for freight. Due to the carrier's lax bookkeeping, however, the feed supply first learned of the processor's practice on the eleventh delivery, when the carrier billed the feed supply for eleven freight charges. The feed supply objected immediately. The processor's nonpayment of the freight is not a course of performance because the feed supply never knowingly acquiesced. If, however, the feed supply had willingly paid the freight on the first ten deliveries, a course of performance, implying an agreement that the feed supply company would pay for freight on subsequent deliveries, might well have been established.

- -

Course of Dealing.   Terms can also be supplied to a contract through the parties' prior course of dealing. In contrast with the parties' course of performance, the parties' course of dealing is the sequence of conduct between the parties before the formation of the contract at issue, and unrelated to that contract, which establishes a common understanding between them for interpreting their expressions and other conduct relating to the contract at issue. Rev. § 1-303(b).

- -

> EXAMPLE 2: A brewer contracted to sell and deliver to a wholesaler 50,000 gallons of "pale ale" each year for five years. The contract stated a price per gallon but made no provision for future changes in price or quantity due to fluctuating market influences. Under past contracts

between the brewer and the wholesaler for the sale of similar products, there have been repeated and substantial deviations from the amounts and prices stated in the contracts when market declines occurred. Three years after formation of the instant contract, the price of pale ale plummeted. The wholesaler, who could not resell the ale at competitive prices, asked the brewer to reduce the price for further deliveries to current market levels as was done in the past. The brewer refused and the wholesaler did not accept future deliveries. In response to the brewer's suit for breach, the wholesaler will likely be allowed to introduce evidence of the past deviations to establish a common basis of understanding for interpreting the disputed contract.

The most common situation where course of dealing will apply is where the parties have engaged in a series of contracts similar to the disputed contract.

Usage of Trade.   The terms of a contract also can be found through usage of trade. The Code defines "usage of trade" in Rev. § 1-303(c) as "any practice or method of dealing having such regularity of observance in a place, vocation, or trade as to justify an expectation that it will be observed with respect to the transaction in question." The purpose behind making usage of trade admissible for purposes of interpreting a contract is that if a certain practice is common in the trade, the contracting parties, knowing of the practice and assuming its existence, might not have thought about adding it to the memorialized agreement but nonetheless assumed that the practice controlled the agreement of the parties.

EXAMPLE 3: A poultry farmer contracted to sell to a stew manufacturer 50,000 tons annually of "U.S. Fresh Frozen Chicken." The stew manufacturer's new purchasing agent, who had no experience in the specific area of stew manufacturing, agreed to the contract. It was commonly understood in the stew trade that the term "chicken" meant "young chicken suitable only for broiling, frying, or roasting." In the stew manufacturer's suit against the poultry farmer for delivery of inferior chicken unsuitable for stewing, the poultry farmer will be allowed to introduce evidence of the trade meaning of "chicken" to establish an understanding for interpreting the disputed contract term of which the stew manufacturer should have been aware.

Trade usage may be admissible, regardless of whether one of the parties to the contract is aware of the trade usage at issue, because knowledge of trade usage can be imputed to parties. Trade usage may be used to supplement or qualify the terms of an agreement so long as the parties either are aware or should be aware of the usage. Rev. § 1-303(c). The main requirement is whether there is a "regularity of observance" in the trade. The Code's standard for trade usage—that a usage be repetitive and lawful—is far less demanding than the common law requirements for "custom," which usually require that a usage be reasonable, lawful, well known, certain, precise, universal, ancient, and continuous. *See* Rev. § 1-303, Official Comment 3. Whether the proffered evidence is usage of the trade in which the parties are involved is a question of fact.

3. FILLING THE GAPS: DEFAULT TERMS

The parties' agreement including the express terms, course of performance, course of dealing, and usage of trade may not contain all of the terms necessary to determine parties' obligations in performance of the contract. To deal with these situations, Article 2 has adopted various "gap-filling" provisions. These default terms are incorporated into the contract to fill the missing gaps. The most important of these gap-filling rules are discussed below.

Price.   Although the absence of a price term in the contract may suggest that no intent existed to form a binding contract by one or both of the parties, Article 2 makes it clear that parties can form a contract without a price term. Rev. § 2-305(1). A price term may be absent in a contract either because the parties failed to mention a price term or because they agreed to decide the price term later but did not do so. In either case, the price will be a reasonable price measured at the time of delivery. Rev. § 2-305(1)(a)–(b).

Another reason the parties may not have specified a contract price term is that they anticipated that a third party would designate the term or that the price would be fixed by an external agreed-upon standard. In either case, a reasonable price will be imposed if the price term is not ultimately set by these means, so long as proof of the requisite intent to form a contract is evident. Rev. § 2-305(1)(c).

Either the buyer or the seller may reserve the right to set the contract price, but the party must set the price in good faith. Rev. § 2-305(2). If the right to set the contract price is reserved to one of the contracting parties and no price is fixed because of the fault of one of the parties, the other party may treat the contract as canceled or fix a reasonable price. Rev. § 2-305(3).

Where the parties did not intend to form a binding contract unless a price term could ultimately be agreed to, and no agreement was reached, there is no contract and the buyer must return any goods received. Rev. § 2-305(4). The buyer, if unable to return the goods, must pay the goods' reasonable value at the time of delivery. *Id.* If the buyer returns the goods, the seller must return any portion of the price that was paid on account. *Id.*

EXAMPLE 4: A seller agreed to supply a buyer with a shipment of 1,000 reams of high-quality bond paper. Nothing was said as to the price. The seller shipped the paper to the buyer. The buyer decided it did not want to take the paper due to a change in the buyer's paper needs. If the parties did not intend to contract without setting a price, then there was no contract and the buyer need not accept the goods but should return them to the seller. If the parties intended to contract even though price was not agreed to, the price will be a reasonable price at the time of delivery.

Delivery. Article 2 provides terms for the manner, place, and time for delivery absent express agreement. Unless the parties agree otherwise, the tender of goods is required in a single delivery. § 2-307. The circumstances may give either contracting party the right to make or demand delivery in lots. In this case, the price may be demanded upon delivery of each lot if the price can be apportioned among the deliveries.

> **EXAMPLE 5:** A seller and a buyer agreed that the seller will supply the buyer 5,000 telephones for use in a new office building. The presumption under § 2-307 is that those 5,000 telephones will be made in a single delivery. Assume, however, that the seller knew that the 5,000 telephones would not be needed all at once as the building was going to be occupied in stages over the course of several months. In addition, the buyer has informed the seller that the buyer had very limited storage space. Those circumstances may be sufficient to indicate delivery in lots is acceptable.

The place of delivery, if none is provided for in the agreement, is the seller's place of business, or if none, the seller's residence. Rev. § 2-308(a). Thus, the presumption is that the buyer will pick up the goods from the seller. If, however, the contract is for the sale of identified goods that are known to be located in some other place, that place will be the required place of delivery. Rev. § 2-308(b). If no term concerning time of delivery is included in the contract, goods must be delivered within a reasonable time. Rev. § 2-309(1). The rules governing the performance of the tender of delivery are discussed in Chapter 6.

Payment.   Generally, payment is due at the point where the buyer is to receive the goods rather than the point where the seller is obligated to deliver the goods. Rev. § 2-310(a). This distinction between the place of receipt and the place of delivery provides the buyer with a right of preliminary inspection of the goods on delivery before the buyer must pay. Rev. § 2-513. Thus, even when goods are considered delivered upon shipment, the buyer need not pay for the goods until it receives, and has an opportunity to inspect, the goods. This ability to inspect prior to payment is discussed further in Chapter 6.

Other Terms Regarding Performance.   Article 2 has a catchall provision to cover other gaps in the parties' agreement about performance of the contract. Failure to make a specification about performance at contract formation does not prevent the contract from being formed. Rev. § 2-311(1). Particulars of performance not specified when the contract is formed may be specified by one of the parties thereafter. A specification made later must be made in good faith and be commercially reasonable. Rev. § 2-311(1). Revised § 2-311 provides a presumption that buyers are to specify the assortment of the goods and sellers are to specify shipment arrangements. Rev. § 2-311(2).

4. Issues with Output, Requirement, and Exclusive Dealings Contract Terms

A requirements contract is an agreement under which the buyer agrees to purchase goods to meet its "requirements" for those goods. In contrast, an output contract is an agreement under which the seller agrees to sell all of the specified goods that the seller distributes. In both cases, there is no "set" quantity term. Quantity is measured solely by the buyer's requirements or the seller's output. In the past, these forms of agreements were often struck down as being illusory because one party had no definite obligation to sell or buy any amount of goods.

Article 2 recognizes the validity of both output and requirements contracts as containing a sufficiently definite quantity of goods to allow enforcement of the contract. At the same time,

Article 2 places restrictions upon the buyer and seller with regard to these types of contracts and, in particular, specifies that the obligation to set requirements or outputs must be performed in good faith. § 2-306(1). These obligations, to buy what is in good faith required or to sell what is in good faith the actual output, effectively restrain the parties from refusing to buy or sell unless that refusal is based on a good faith reason.

- -

> EXAMPLE 6: A producer contracted to sell to a utility all of the natural gas that the utility required to fulfill the current utility needs of its customers. The contract was effective for ten years and made no provision for future changes in price due to fluctuating market influences. This requirements contract is enforceable under § 2-306(1). The utility has the obligation in good faith to buy what is required to meet that need. Two years after contract formation, the market price of natural gas rose significantly. Within two months, the utility's demand for gas—which had remained nearly constant during the two-year period—escalated by nearly fifty percent. Six months later, the producer lawfully obtained evidence that the utility was stockpiling gas in its facilities for future use as well as reselling gas to a neighboring city whose supply contract with the producer expired recently. The producer refused to supply the utility's demands. In defense against the utility's suit, the producer would likely avoid liability because the utility's demands did not, in good faith, appear to serve the original purpose of the contract, i.e., fulfilling the current natural gas needs of the utility's customers.

- -

By including an estimate in the contract, a buyer or seller can limit its risk by placing a more finite limit upon the quantity of goods that can be tendered or demanded. If the parties state an estimate, the requirements or outputs must not be unreasonably disproportionate to that estimate. § 2-306(1). Optimally, the parties may choose to include in the contract a minimum or maximum quantity that can be tendered or demanded to prevent one or the other party from being forced contractually out of business.

An additional restriction is triggered where the parties have provided no stated estimate. Demands or tenders, though made in good faith, cannot be unreasonably disproportionate to any normal or otherwise comparable prior output or requirements. § 2-306(1). This limits the risks of the parties to the contract by making it clear that when no estimates are available, the court may consider past deliveries to determine if the parties had contemplated limitations upon the quantity of goods that can be demanded or tendered. In Example 6, the utility's previous requirements also could be used to determine if its demanded requirements were reasonable.

An exclusive dealings contract is an agreement under which the seller or buyer agrees to contract solely with the other party in a specified area of business. Such contracts are most common in distributorship arrangements where the seller of goods gives the buyer exclusive rights to resell the product but sets no quantity. In this type of contract, Article 2 implies a "best effort" term in the contract. In an exclusive dealings contract, the seller is obligated to use its best efforts to supply the goods and the buyer is obligated to use its best efforts to promote their sale. § 2-306(2). This requirement places a stringent burden on a party to produce or sell goods because that party should comprehend that the other party is relying exclusively on these efforts. For example, if a seller agrees to an exclusive contract with a buyer who agrees to distribute the goods, the buyer has a duty to use its best efforts to promote distribution of the goods. This provides the seller, whose success is in the sole hands of the buyer, with a greater degree of protection. This standard applies with equal force in contracts under which the buyer has been given the exclusive right to sell the seller's goods in a specified territory.

5. RESOLVING CONFLICTS IN TERMS

With so many factors to be considered in finding the terms of an agreement, the question of how to resolve conflicts in terms often arises. Revised § 1-303(e) deals with the resolution of these conflicts as between express terms, course of performance, course of dealing, and usage of trade. If the express terms cannot be construed as consistent with these implied terms, the basic hierarchy of terms is that express terms trump terms implied by course of performance, course of dealing, and usage of trade. Course of performance terms trump course of dealing and usage of trade terms, and course of dealing terms trump usage of trade terms. Rev. § 1-303(e). Thus, extrinsic evidence that explains or supplements express terms with which that evidence is consistent should be considered in the following order: course of performance, course of dealing, and usage of trade. If the express terms and extrinsic evidence are inconsistent, then the express terms will control. Only if there are gaps left after considering these sources of terms should the Article 2 "gap fillers" be consulted to determine the parties' obligations.

B. CONTRACT INTERPRETATION

Even if the contract terms are expressly agreed to by the parties, those terms may need to be interpreted. The line between contract interpretation and filling in the gaps in an agreement in many instances may be hard to discern. Both interpretation and "gap filling" are designed to ascertain what the parties intended to happen in the course of performing this contract. To that end, the Code prescribes that course of performance, course of dealing, and usage of trade are to be used not only to fill in the gaps but also to help interpret the parties' expression of the terms of their agreement. Rev. § 1-303(d). This focus on the commercial context of the agreement rejects the "plain meaning rule" used at common law for interpretation of terms of an agreement. That common law rule provided that the court should ascertain the "plain meaning" of the words in the agreement. Under Article 2, however, the court would look to the relevant course of performance, course of dealing, and usage of trade to determine the meaning of the words of the agreement.

EXAMPLE 7: In Example 3, the issue of whether the contract was for the sale of stewing chickens or chickens
meant for other purposes could be treated as one of contract interpretation. Usage of trade would be relevant to
demonstrate whether the word "chicken" in the contract
meant "stewing chicken." A plain meaning approach
to interpretation of the term "chicken" might focus on
whether the proffered poultry was a chicken as opposed
to a duck or a turkey.

Other common law rules of interpretation that are not displaced
by a provision in Article 2 would supplement Article 2's interpretation rule that uses course of performance, course of dealing, and
usage of trade to interpret the terms in the agreement. Rev. § 1-103.
One of the Article 2 sections that does influence what evidence
may be used to interpret the agreement is the parol evidence rule.

C. PAROL EVIDENCE RULE

As demonstrated above, even though the parties have formed a
contract, oftentimes a court must ascertain the terms and meaning of that contract. The parol evidence rule is a tool that is used
to determine what evidence is admissible in ascertaining the
terms of a contract and their meaning when the parties' agreement is in a record. The parol evidence rule arose in the common
law interpretation of written contracts to prevent introduction of
evidence that contradicted or varied the terms contained in the
written document.

To understand the parol evidence rule, one must make a distinction between the parties' agreement and the paper document or
record on which the agreement or a part of the agreement may be
memorialized. Although it is common usage to refer to the contract
as the paper document, the "contract" as defined in the Code is the
"total legal obligation [of the parties] that results from the parties'
agreement" and applicable rules of law. Rev. § 1-201(b)(12). The

parties' agreement is the "bargain in fact" as found in their language or in applicable course of performance, course of dealing, and usage of trade. Rev. § 1-201(b)(3). Neither of these definitions contemplates that the agreement or the contract will be in a record. The only section of Article 2 that contemplates a record requirement is the statute of frauds, Rev. § 2-201. As explained previously, that record need not be, and often is not, a record that embodies all of the terms of the parties' agreement or contract.

The parol evidence rule is based upon the idea that if the evidence of an agreement is in a record, that record is a better indication of the parties' actual agreement in some circumstances. The rule has been criticized because it allows judges to weigh the credibility of evidence and choose what is actually submitted to the trier of fact regarding the alleged contract terms and their meaning. In some cases, the rule can operate to prevent credible evidence of the parties' intent regarding their agreement from reaching the finder of fact.

Revised § 2-202 embodies Article 2's version of the parol evidence rule. This section does not apply to every record containing terms that are alleged to be part of the contract. Revised § 2-202 only applies when one of two fact situations is present. The first situation is when there are "terms with respect to which the confirmatory records of the parties agree." Rev. § 2-202. The second situation is when "terms . . . which are otherwise set forth in a record intended by the parties as a final expression of their agreement with respect to such terms as are included therein." *Id.* If one of those two situations exists, then Rev. § 2-202 applies and those terms included in the record may not be "contradicted by evidence of any prior agreement or of a contemporaneous oral agreement." *Id.* Both of these situations could exist as to either a totally integrated agreement (the parties have placed all of their terms in a record) or a partially integrated agreement (the parties have placed some, but not all, of their terms in a record).

EXAMPLE 8: A retailer ordered 100 stereos from a manufacturer over the phone. The parties agreed orally to a price and delivery terms. Each sent to the other a confirmation of the order stating accurately the price, quantity, and delivery terms. As to those three terms, the confirming records of the parties agreed and could not be contradicted by evidence of a prior agreement or a contemporaneous oral agreement. This is an example of a partially integrated agreement. The parties have not discussed or agreed to any other terms such as warranty, payment method, and time of payment.

EXAMPLE 9: A manufacturer and a retailer signed one record that set forth the price, quantity, and delivery terms for stereos. This record was signed after extensive negotiation of those three terms. If a court finds that the record was intended as the final expression of the parties' agreement as to those three terms, those three terms could not be contradicted by evidence of any prior agreement or a contemporaneous oral agreement. This also is an example of a partially integrated agreement.

In both examples, the terms in the records may be explained or supplemented by course of performance, course of dealing, and usage of trade. Rev. § 2-202(a). As explained previously, this is true even if those two fact situations do not exist. The definition of "agreement" and the statutory sections on those three terms all provide that the parties' agreed terms can be explained and supplemented by course of performance, course of dealing , and usage of trade. The provisions of the parol evidence rule in Rev. § 2-202 do not change that basic concept of supplementation and interpretation with that type of evidence.

If Rev. § 2-202 applies, the section also provides that the terms in those records may be explained or supplemented by evidence of "consistent additional terms." Rev. § 2-202(1)(b). The only time that those consistent additional terms cannot be put into evidence is when the parties intended the record not only to be a final expression of their agreement on the terms in the record but also to be a "complete and exclusive statement of the terms the agreement." If the parties intend the record to contain all of the terms of the agreement, the record is totally integrated. Even if the parties intended a totally integrated agreement, however, evidence of course of performance, course of dealing, and usage of trade can still be used to explain or supplement the terms in the record.

Article 2 provides little guidance for determining whether the parties intended a record to be completely or partially integrated. One piece of evidence that parties often use to show the intent to completely integrate the agreement is a merger clause. A merger clause is a clause in a record that explicitly states that the terms in the record constitute the entire agreement of the parties. A merger clause in the record may or may not be conclusive as to whether the parties intended the record to be a fully integrated agreement. Rev. § 2-202, Official Comment 3. Some courts hold that merger clauses are conclusive on the issue of the parties' intent to integrate the agreement; other courts look at the surrounding circumstances in addition to the merger clause to determine the parties' intent.

EXAMPLE 10: In a record, a manufacturer and a retailer agreed to price, quantity, and delivery terms. The parties provided nothing in the record about the manner in which the price was to be paid. The record stated that it was a "final, complete, and exclusive statement of the parties' agreement." Prior to signing the record, the retailer and the manufacturer had allegedly agreed that the retailer would send a certified check sixty days after delivery of the goods. The manufacturer, in its action to receive payment for the goods, argues that the absence of an express payment term means that payment was due when the retailer received the goods under the gap-filler provision of Rev. § 2-310. The retailer counters that the parties had a prior agreement for a sixty-day credit. Under Rev. § 2-202, the issue is whether the merger clause and other evidence convince the court that the parties intended to have a fully integrated agreement. That other evidence could be discussions of the parties, the prior course of dealing between the parties, and the usual practice in the trade. If it was a fully integrated agreement, then the alleged term regarding payment sixty days later is not allowed into evidence. If the merger clause and other evidence did not convince the court that the agreement was totally integrated—that is, that it was only partially integrated—the issue is whether the payment term discussed is a "consistent additional term" or whether it is evidence of a prior agreement that contradicts the terms in the record. The record is silent as to the time of payment so the prior discussion should not be construed to be contradictory and could be a consistent additional term.

Non-statutory exceptions to the parol evidence rule may be used by a court to allow in evidence other terms. For example, some courts have found that a party may not invoke the parol evidence rule to shield its own fraud. Parol evidence has also been permitted to show mutual or unilateral mistake.

D. OTHER LIMITATIONS ON CONTRACT ENFORCEMENT

1. UNCONSCIONABILITY

Parties to a contract are generally free to set the terms of the bargain. Courts, however, have placed some limits on the enforcement of some terms in extreme cases. The doctrine of unconscionability is an example of one mechanism that courts sometimes employ to limit the enforcement of a contract or contract terms. Article 2 addresses this concept in Rev. § 2-302. If the court finds that a contract or one of its terms is unconscionable, it may choose one of three remedies. First, the court may refuse to enforce the entire contract. Rev. § 2-302(1). Second, the court may decide not to enforce an unconscionable clause but still enforce the remainder of the contract. *Id.* Third, the court may limit, but not negate, the application of the unconscionable clause in the contract. *Id.*

Although Rev. § 2-302 does little to define which particular type of agreement or clause may be unconscionable, its Official Comment sets out guiding principles for courts to follow in analyzing an unconscionability claim. Subsequent to the Code's initial adoption by the states, a general approach evolved. There are two generally accepted aspects of unconscionability: procedural and substantive.

Procedural Unconscionability. This aspect of unconscionability involves those objective aspects of the bargain which appear to create an absence of any meaningful choice by the disadvantaged party. Courts will review whether a party used fine print to hide contract terms, exercised disparate or unequal bargaining power, or abused an obvious lack of understanding on the part of the other party.

EXAMPLE 11: An uneducated mother of seven with a fixed annual income of $11,000 entered a complex installment contract with an electronics dealership. The contract's cross-collateralization clause, which is printed in very fine, pale print on the record's back side, provided that each of the buyer's payments would be credited pro rata to all purchases which the buyer had ever made from the dealer's store. Effectively, this meant that until the buyer's outstanding balance reached zero, the dealer retained a security interest in every item the buyer had ever bought from the dealer. The buyer bought $1,800 worth of goods from the dealer under the contract. After the buyer paid almost $1,500, she defaulted and the dealer attempted to repossess all of the purchased items. The buyer's lack of education, combined with the dealer's unsavory tactic of burying the cross-collateralization clause in boilerplate language, may render the contract procedurally unconscionable.

Procedural unconscionability alone, however, is not generally fatal to an agreement, because this aspect on its own does not typically show that the bargain was in fact unfair.

Substantive Unconscionability. This aspect of unconscionability goes to the question of the bargain's actual fairness. "The basic test is whether, in light of the general commercial background and the commercial needs of the particular trade or case, the term or contract involved are so one-sided as to be unconscionable under the circumstances existing at the time of the making of the contract." Rev. § 2-302, Official Comment 1. Article 2 specifies that one particular type of contract clause, dealing with limitations of remedies, will generally be considered substantively unconscionable. Section 2-719(3) provides in part that "limitation of consequential damages for injury to the person in the case of consumer goods is prima facie unconscionable but limitation of damages where the loss is commercial is not." The courts have not resolved how a seller is to overcome this presumption. The most common terms found to be substantively unconscionable are excessive contract price terms.

EXAMPLE 12: A homeowner contracted with a seller to have the seller supply and install windows and aluminum siding on the homeowner's home. The goods and services had a market value of $1,000 (for purposes of this example, presume that the goods aspects predominate). However, when the seller's "commission" and "finance charges" were added, the total contract price reached $3,600. The excessive price term may be substantively unconscionable.

Though some courts have held that to support a finding of unconscionability under former § 2-302, both procedural and substantive unconscionability must be present, other courts require only a finding of substantive unconscionability. This approach was not changed in the 2003 amendments. The question of unconscionability clearly is a matter of law that the court, not a jury, must decide. Consequently, an unconscionability claim is reviewed de novo on appeal.

Unconscionability must exist at the time the contract is formed. Courts generally will not find the agreement unconscionable if the bargain was fair for both parties at its inception. Parties may bring in evidence of the commercial setting, purpose, and intended effect of the contract to assist the court in analyzing an unconscionability claim. Rev. § 2-203(2).

2. MODIFICATION AND WAIVER

Modification. When the parties agree to change a contract term after the agreement is initially formed, there is a contract modification. To apply Rev. § 2-209, one must demonstrate that a contract was formed and that the parties have agreed to change one or more of those original terms. The common law rule is that for a contract to be modified, the modification must be supported by consideration. Attempted modifications of one party's obligations were often not supported by consideration because the other party was merely performing its preexisting obligation. At common law, the obligation to perform a preexisting duty is not consideration for the proposed modification. Article 2 changes this rule, eliminating the consideration requirement. Rev. § 2-209(1). Official Comment 2 to Rev. § 2-209 treats good faith as a substitute for consideration. "Good faith" means "honesty in fact" and "observance of reasonable commercial standards of fair dealing." Rev. § 2-103(1)(j). The good faith obligation is thus used to determine whether an agreement to modify is enforceable.

One party's mere proposal of a modification does not result in an agreement to modify. Official Comment 2 to Rev. § 2-209 suggests that a party must act in good faith and have a legitimate commercial reason in order to seek a contract modification. This comment suggests the courts should police against "forced modifications." A forced modification may occur because the party to whom the proposal to modify is made may not have any real choice in the matter given that party's circumstances at the time the proposal is made. A party with no real choice in the matter may not have agreed to the modification proposed.

EXAMPLE 13: A seller contracted to sell 100 stereos to a buyer by November 15 in exchange for $10,000. Later, the seller proposed to the buyer that the seller deliver the stereos on October 1 or not at all. The buyer did not want the stereos that early because the buyer did not have the storage capacity and did not want to pay someone else to store the stereos until the holiday buying season when the buyer expects to have a big demand for these items. If the buyer rejects the proposal to modify, the seller will breach the contract and the buyer will be unable to get stereos from anyone else in time for the holiday season. The seller's proposal to modify must be made in good faith and for a legitimate commercial reason in order to protect the buyer from the seller's attempt to extort a modification. On the other hand, if the buyer wants to agree to such a modification, then the buyer may do so. The seller need provide no additional consideration to the buyer for the modification to be binding on them both.

Often litigated is whether a contract modification must be in a record when there is a "no-oral-modification" clause in the agreement. A no-oral-modification clause is a clause that provides that any modifications to the agreement must be in a record. Under the common law, no-oral-modification clauses were usually considered unenforceable on the premise that the parties could always change their minds later. Article 2 specifically changes this result. If the parties desire to impose the requirement of a record upon themselves, the parties may incorporate an enforceable no-oral-modification clause into the agreement. Rev. § 2-209(2). Where a no-oral-modification clause is contained in a record provided by a merchant party to a nonmerchant party, the record containing the clause must be signed separately by the nonmerchant for the provision to be enforceable. *Id.* If both parties are merchants, the "separate signing" requirement does not apply. *Id.*

Absent a contrary agreement between the parties, "[t]he requirements of Section 2-201 must be satisfied if the contract as modified is within its provisions." Rev. § 2-209(3). It is unclear precisely what this provision demands. Scholars have observed that this requires, generally, a modification in a record that satisfies Rev. § 2-201 if the modified term (1) brings the entire contract within Rev. § 2-201 for the first time—for example, if the price is raised from $4,500 to $5,500, (2) falls within Rev. § 2-201 on its own—for example, if the price term is raised from $5,500 to $6,500, or (3) alters the quantity term of a contract originally within Rev. § 2-201—for example, if the quantity is raised from 100 to 200. *See* Chapter 2 Section E.2. It is less certain whether any modification must satisfy Rev. § 2-201 solely because the original contract fell within Rev. § 2-201.

An exception to either the parties' no-oral-modification clause (i.e., a "private" statute of frauds) or the enacted (i.e., "public") statute of frauds requirement is set out in Rev. § 2-209(4), which states, "[a]lthough an attempt at modification or rescission does not satisfy the requirements of subsections (2) or (3) it may operate as a waiver." Such a purported modification may be the result either of an oral agreement, when the parties contracted for no oral modifications, or of the parties' course of performance inasmuch as it is inconsistent with the terms of the contract contained in a record.

Waiver.   Construed broadly, Rev. § 2-209(4) provides that any attempted modification that does not meet the requirement of a record is still enforceable under a theory of waiver. A "waiver" is commonly defined as "an intentional relinquishment of a known right." Generally, waivers do not need consideration or reliance to be enforceable. If any attempt at a modification not in compliance with subsections (2) or (3) could be a waiver, those subsections would be effectively nullified. Revised § 2-209(5) sets out when and how a waiver of an executory portion of a contract may be retracted. A waiver may be retracted so long as the retraction would not be unjust in light of any material change of position made by the nonretracting party in reliance on the waiver. Rev. § 2-209(5). Moreover, the retracting party must provide reasonable notification to the other party that strict performance of any term waived previously will be required. *Id.*

Revised § 2-209(5) is consistent with an interpretation of Rev. § 2-209(4) that mixes reliance with waiver so that a term may be waived and that waiver is enforced if the other party relied on that waiver to their detriment.

- -

EXAMPLE 14: A buyer contracted to buy, from a seller, dies to be used in the buyer's manufacturing plant. Under the contract, all modifications must be in a record and signed by the buyer to be enforceable. The seller told the buyer that the delivery would be late and the buyer orally agreed. The seller later shipped the goods and the buyer accepted the late delivery. In response to the buyer's suit for breach, the seller contended that the buyer's conduct manifested agreement to delivery on the later dates and thus the buyer waived the no-oral-modification clause. If the seller could show detrimental reliance on the buyer's conduct (such as by demonstrating an ability to ship on the original date but failing to do so because of buyer's agreement to late shipment) many courts would hold that the buyer's conduct waived the no-oral-modification clause. If, conversely, the seller could not show detrimental reliance, the no-oral-modification clause would remain effective and the agreement's original delivery term would be enforced.

- -

That leaves a basic issue of whether the Code drafters have confused estoppel with waiver. In estoppel, the focus is on reasonably detrimental reliance on another party's conduct or words in order to preclude the other party from enforcing rights inconsistent with the conduct or words. Estoppel principles supplement Article 2 under Rev. § 1-103, which makes one wonder what subsections (4) and (5) are designed to do. Needless to say, the cases in this area are very confusing and inconsistent.

CHAPTER

FOUR

CONTRACT TERMS: EXPRESS AND IMPLIED WARRANTIES

A contract for the sale of goods may contain many different types of express or implied terms. Some of those terms were discussed in Chapter 3. This chapter discusses express and implied warranty terms that may become part of a contract for sale. In a contract for sale, the parties have expectations about the quality of the goods. Those expectations form the basis of the idea of "warranty." As stated in Official Comment 6 to Rev. § 2-313, "[t]he whole purpose of the law of warranty is to determine what it is that the seller has in essence agreed to sell." Those warranties—expectations based upon what the seller has agreed to sell—may arise from what is said (express warranty), from the conduct of the parties during the sales transaction (implied warranty of fitness for a particular purpose), or from notice of the type of transaction (implied warranty of merchantability). When discussing warranty terms, just as with other terms discussed in Chapter 3, the same two questions must be answered: (1) What is the warranty term and what does it mean? and (2) Did the warranty term become part of the parties' agreement? The answer to this second question will often depend upon the validity of a disclaimer term in the parties' agreement.

Sections 2-312 through 2-315 set out Article 2's warranty provisions and establish two broad categories of warranties, express and implied. Revised § 2-313 governs express warranties. Two new sections, 2-313A and 2-313B, govern express warranty type obligations to remote purchasers. The remaining sections set forth and govern implied warranties, which are imposed by law on sellers without regard to the representations made during or after contract formation. These implied warranties become part of the parties' "total legal obligation"—the contract. Rev. § 1-201(b)(12).

A. EXPRESS WARRANTIES

Revised § 2-313 addresses express warranties which arise from the seller's affirmative actions. An "express warranty" is any of the following which become part of the "basis of the bargain": (1) an affirmation of fact or promise made by the seller that relates to the goods, (2) descriptions of the goods, or (3) samples and models. Rev. § 2-313(2). No formal terms of guarantee need be employed, and the seller's subjective intent to warrant the goods is not relevant. Rev. § 2-313(3). Express warranties under Rev. § 2-313 are limited to privity relationships between buyers and sellers, and to emphasize that point Rev. § 2-313 now provides a definition of "immediate buyer." Rev. § 2-313(1). Nonprivity express warranty type obligations are provided for by the new §§ 2-313A and 2-313B.

Basis of the Bargain and Reliance. Under pre-Code commercial law, to prove an enforceable express warranty, buyers bore the burden of proving that they actually relied on the seller's representations. The Code requires only that a seller's representations become "part of the basis of the bargain" but provides no specific definition of this requirement. One of the most rigorous debates in warranty law concerns whether Article 2 "basis of the bargain" analysis supplants, or conversely, incorporates the pre-Code requirement of reliance. Some authorities argue that Article 2 eliminates reliance as a factor of an express warranty. Others contend that Article 2's silence on the issue reflects a lack of intent to change the pre-Code law. Official Comment 5 to former and Rev. § 2-313 provides:

> In actual practice affirmations of fact made by the seller about the goods during a bargain are regarded as part of the description of the goods; hence no particular reliance on such statements need be shown in order to weave them into the fabric of the agreement. Rather, any fact which is to take these affirmations, once made, out of the agreement requires clear affirmative proof.

The predominate view is to interpret this Official Comment as establishing a rebuttable presumption of reliance that sellers must disprove. In practice, most courts still find the reliance by the buyer on the seller's express warranty of some significance, although courts vary on which party has the burden to prove the reliance or lack of it.

EXAMPLE 1: A seller advertised hair dye that is guaranteed to last three times longer than a competing brand (which lasts one month). A buyer saw the advertisement but bought the dye because he liked the color. When the hair dye washed out within one week after using it, the buyer sought to get his money back. Even though the buyer did not rely on the representation about how long the hair dye would last, that representation became part of the basis of the bargain and what the seller agreed to sell.

----

1. PROMISES RELATING TO THE GOODS AND AFFIRMATIONS OF FACT

Promises and affirmations of facts that are made by sellers and that relate to the characteristics and utility of goods may be binding as warranties. Rev. § 2-313(2)(a). These representations must be made to the buyer. Revised § 2-313(3) provides for broad application of this principle by dispensing with the need for formal language.

Revised § 2-313 also provides that a seller's statement of commendation or opinion does not create a warranty. Courts uniformly adopted this principle in theory, but the standards employed to distinguish promises and affirmations of fact from opinions are not uniform. Courts will often consider the following to determine whether a statement constitutes an opinion:

- the specificity of the statement;
- the context in which the statement was made;
- the nature of the defect;
- the parties' relative knowledge and sophistication;
- the language employed by the seller; and
- whether the statement was written or oral.

As with all warranty claims, these cases are fact sensitive. Indistinguishable fact patterns often produce dissimilar results in different courts. The weight accorded each factor varies among courts, and no one factor normally will be dispositive.

EXAMPLE 2: A buyer, with no knowledge about cars, contracted to buy a new car from a dealer who was aware of the buyer's lack of knowledge about cars. Upon the advice of her friends, the buyer asked the dealer whether the engine was the largest available for that model of car. The dealer replied that the engine "is an eight cylinder, the best engine available." Three months later, when the buyer had the oil in the car changed, she discovered that the engine was in fact only a six-cylinder engine. The dealer's statement that the car had eight cylinders was an express warranty. The representation about whether it was the best engine available could be merely a commendation or opinion of the seller.

----

2. DESCRIPTIONS OF THE GOODS

Descriptions of the goods by either the buyer or seller may create express warranties. Rev. § 2-313(2)(b). Though descriptions often appear indistinguishable from affirmations of fact, descriptions may be broader than affirmations of fact to the extent that descriptive terms include symbols that have special meaning within the context of particular transactions.

EXAMPLE 3: A buyer bought a pesticide from a seller. The product's packaging bore the emblem "EPA." The buyer believed that the product, which later damaged his yard, had received EPA approval. If a court agreed that the letters "EPA" could symbolize compliance with EPA requirements, the descriptive letters would be the basis for an express warranty even though the seller never affirmatively stated that the product met EPA standards. The packaging also contained a list of all of the chemicals enclosed. That list is a description of the product and also an affirmation of fact about what the package contained.

The buyer may also make a description. For example, a buyer may request a product of a certain description and the seller may furnish that product. For example, assume the buyer requested forty-weight oil and the oil the seller furnishes is twenty-weight oil. The buyer's request is a description that the seller adopted by purporting to supply goods meeting that description.

Often, parties concede that a term is descriptive but contest the meaning of the description. Courts rely on many of the same factors used to distinguish affirmation from opinion to make this determination of meaning. Generic terms that appear in descriptions often prove troubling because they may be construed very narrowly or broadly. One court may decide, for example, that "car" means "a combination of plastic and metal that is mobile" while another court may decide that it means "a product that provides the amenities and performs the functions that a buyer could expect reasonably from a product designed to provide transportation."

3. SAMPLES OR MODELS

Samples or models used by sellers during the course of bargaining may also create express warranties. Rev. § 2-313(2)(c). An often-litigated issue under this section is whether the sample or model established a standard of quality that the seller guaranteed to meet. Courts look first at whether the parties acted as if the sample or model connoted such a standard and then look to trade usage and custom to make this determination. Although Official Comment 8 to Rev. § 2-313 suggests that courts should presume that anything illustrative of goods is a standard-creating sample or model unless the seller states expressly that the delivered goods will be of a grade inferior to that of the proffered sample, not all courts have elected to follow this suggestion.

- -

> EXAMPLE 4: A buyer went to a warehouse operated by a grain processor to purchase five tons of grain. The processor sent the buyer into a storage area where a five-ton pile of grain was located. The processor made no oral or written representations about the nature of the grain. The buyer contracted to buy five tons of grain to be delivered a week later. The processor delivered five tons of grain that had greater moisture content than the grain the buyer observed. The issue would be whether the five-ton pile was a sample or model resulting in an express warranty that the grain contracted for would conform to the sample or model.

- -

A "sample" is a unit "drawn from the bulk of goods which is the subject matter of the sale." Rev. § 2-313, Official Comment 8. Conversely, a "model" is "offered for inspection when the subject matter is not at hand and which has not been drawn from the bulk of the goods" that is the subject of the sale. *Id.* Samples are considered more representative of quality standards than are models because samples have an obviously closer nexus to the goods that ultimately change hands.

4. REMEDIAL PROMISE

Revised § 2-313 introduces the concept of a remedial promise to distinguish between promises made by the seller about how the goods will perform, which are express warranties under Rev. § 2-313, and promises made by the seller about the seller's performance. Rev. § 2-313(4). A "remedial promise" is "a promise by the seller to repair or replace the goods or to refund all or part of the price upon the happening of a specified event." Rev. § 2-103(1)(n). Remedial promises have been separated from promises about the goods themselves in order to fix a statute of limitations problem that occurred when courts erroneously considered a remedial promise to be a warranty and thus allowed the statute of limitations to begin running from the time the goods were tendered and not from the time the seller failed to perform the duty to take the remedial action. Thus, under Rev. § 2-313(4), a remedial promise "creates an obligation that the promise will be performed upon the happening of the specified event," and under Rev. § 2-725, a cause of action for a breach of this obligation arises when the remedial promise is not performed when the performance is due. Rev. § 2-725(2)(c).

B. EXPRESS WARRANTY TYPE OBLIGATION TO REMOTE PURCHASER

Revised Article 2 has two new sections that address express warranty type obligations of sellers to remote purchasers. *See* Rev. §§ 2-313A and 2-313B. Although these sections are similar to Rev. § 2-313 on express warranties, the obligations codified in these sections are referred to not as "warranties" but as "obligations" because, unlike a true warranty, these obligations are not between a direct buyer and seller in a contractual relationship.

These two new sections are limited to "new goods and goods sold or leased as new goods in a transaction of purchase in the normal chain of distribution." Rev. §§ 2-313A(2) & 2-313B(2).

These sections only cover representations that are made to a remote purchaser, defined as "a person that buys or leases goods from an immediate buyer or other person in the normal chain of distribution." Rev. §§ 2-313A(1)(b) & 2-313B(1)(b).

1. REVISED SECTION 2-313A

The seller's obligation under Rev. § 2-313A arises if (1) the seller "makes an affirmation of fact or promise that relates to the goods, provides a description that relates to the goods, or makes a remedial promise," (2) the affirmation, promise, description, or remedial promise is "in a record packaged with or accompanying the goods," and (3) the seller "reasonably expects the record to be, and the record is, furnished to the remote purchaser." Rev. § 2-313A(3).

The seller's obligation to the remote purchaser is that (1) "the goods will conform to the affirmation of fact, promise or description unless a reasonable person in the position of the remote purchaser would not believe that the affirmation of fact, promise or description created an obligation" and (2) the seller "will perform the remedial promise." The distinction between affirmations of fact and an opinion is preserved so that statements that are merely "opinion or commendation of the goods" will not create the obligation. Rev. § 2-313A(4). The seller breaches the obligation created by the affirmation of fact, description, or promise (other than a remedial promise) if the goods did not conform to the affirmation, description, or promise at the time that the goods left the seller's control. Rev. § 2-313A(6). No similar specific rule is provided for when a seller breaches a remedial promise, but a reasonable inference is that a remedial promise is breached at the time that the seller fails to perform the promise.

This section provides several rules that relate to the remedies for a breach of the obligation. First, the seller may modify or limit remedies as long as the modification or limitation is given to the remote purchaser at least by the time of purchase. Rev. § 2-313A(5)(a). The modification or limitation may be included in the same record that provided for the affirmation of fact, promise, or description. *Id.* If the remedy is not modified or limited, the seller is liable for the remote purchaser's incidental and consequential damages under the same tests provided in § 2-715 on buyer's remedies, except that the seller is not liable for a remote purchaser's lost profits. Rev. § 2-313A(5)(b). The measurement of the loss incurred by the remote purchaser may be "determined in any manner that is reasonable." Rev. § 2-313A(5)(c). Official Comment 9 suggests that Rev. § 2-714 provides the appropriate guide for the measurement of the remote purchaser's damages for breach of an obligation, other than a remedial promise, through a comparison of the value of the goods if the seller's obligation had been met and the actual value of the goods.

2. REVISED SECTION 2-313B

Revised § 2-313B follows the same structure as Rev. § 2-313A. However, it differs in that it sets forth the seller's obligation to the remote purchaser for representations made to the public, as opposed to Rev. § 2-313A, which is concerned with representations in records that accompany the goods.

Under Rev. § 2-313B, the seller's obligation arises if (1) the seller "makes an affirmation of fact or promise that relates to the goods, provides a description that relates to the goods, or makes a remedial promise," (2) the affirmation of fact, promise, description, or remedial promise is made "in advertising or a similar communication to the public," and (3) the remote purchaser purchases the goods "with knowledge of and with the expectation that the goods will conform to the affirmation of fact, promise or description, or that the seller will perform the remedial promise." Rev. § 2-313B(3). The seller's obligation to the remote purchaser is that (1) "the goods will conform to the affirmation of fact, promise or description unless a reasonable person in the position of the remote purchaser would not believe that the affirmation of fact, promise or description created an obligation" and (2) that the seller "will perform the remedial promise." *Id.*

Revised § 2-313B also contains the same principles regarding the distinction between affirmations and opinion and regarding remedies as discussed in connection with Rev. § 2-313A. Rev. § 2-313B(4) through (6).

C. IMPLIED WARRANTY OF MERCHANTABILITY

Revised § 2-314 sets out the standards for the creation of the implied warranty of merchantability. This warranty, unless modified or disclaimed, is imposed as a matter of law. The warranty of merchantability is based upon unstated reasonable expectations of the buyer about the quality of the type of goods sold. The merchantability concept is designed to change the common law rule of "caveat emptor." A buyer in a sale of goods transaction has a right to expect that goods from a merchant will meet a certain minimum level of quality. This warranty attaches to all goods sold by merchants with respect to goods of that kind but not to goods sold by nonmerchant sellers or sellers who are merchants due to their skill and knowledge in their occupation. For Rev. § 2-314 purposes, the sale of consumable food products for consumption is expressly deemed to be a sale of goods.

A merchantable product is one that falls within that quality range normally associated by the trade with goods of its type. Though a product of "fair average quality" need not be the best available of its type, it should be better than the worst available. Merchantable goods must be fit for the ordinary purposes for which goods of their description are used, adequately packaged and labeled, and able to pass in the trade without objection. Rev. § 2-314. This list of qualities is not exhaustive. Rev. § 2-314, Official Comment 8. Common sense suggests that the list is susceptible to varying interpretations. Courts often look to the following factors when determining the merchantability of goods:

- the parties' course of performance and dealings;
- trade usage and custom;
- the goods' new or used status;
- the goods' price relative to the market price of similar goods;
- the characteristics and utility of similar brands; and
- relevant government regulations and standards.

The malleable nature of these factors leads to shifting interpretations of "merchantability" over time.

- -

EXAMPLE 5: A buyer purchased a lawn mower from a seller, a lawn and garden supply store. To be merchantable, the lawn mower must "pass without objection in the trade" and be fit for its ordinary purposes. If the lawn mower was unable to cut normal lawn grass, it would be unmerchantable.

EXAMPLE 6: A buyer purchased a lawn mower from his next-door neighbor, a college professor. The neighbor, who is not a merchant, does not make any implied warranty of merchantability. Thus, even if the mower does not cut the grass, the buyer is unable to sue the neighbor for breach of the implied warranty of merchantability.

- -

Official Comment 7 to Rev. § 2-314 states that the test for product defect in tort and merchantability in contract should be the same when recovery is sought for injury to persons and property in both contract and tort. Thus, for example, this comment suggests the following:

[S]uppose that the seller makes a representation about the safety of a lawn mower that becomes part of the basis of the buyer's bargain. The buyer is injured when the gas tank cracks and a fire breaks out. If the lawnmower without the representation is not defective under applicable tort law, it is not unmerchantable under this section. On the other hand, if the lawnmower did not conform to the representation about safety, the seller made and breached an express warranty and the buyer may sue under Article 2.

D. IMPLIED WARRANTY OF FITNESS FOR A PARTICULAR PURPOSE

Section 2-315 recognizes the creation of an implied warranty when a buyer can prove that the seller had reason to know that the buyer relied on the seller's judgment or skill when buying goods for a "particular purpose." This section, which was not changed by the amendments, acknowledges that goods, though merchantable, may not be fit for particular purposes contemplated by the parties. This implied warranty is based upon the idea that a seller who knows a buyer's needs and knows the buyer is relying on the seller to furnish suitable goods has a responsibility to furnish suitable goods.

EXAMPLE 7: A sawmill operator contracted to purchase hydraulic fluid from a dealer. The buyer told the dealer that the buyer wanted to use the fluid in a certain type of saw at the mill. The dealer selected one type of fluid and delivered it to the buyer. Although the fluid would work in most types of industrial saws, it caused frequent breakdowns in the buyer's mill equipment. Though the fluid was merchantable for purposes of Rev. § 2-314, the fluid was not fit for the particular purpose of protecting the buyer's mill equipment. The dealer, knowing the buyer's requirements and knowing that the buyer was relying on the dealer's skill and judgment, has made and breached a warranty of fitness for a particular purpose. If the dealer were a merchant with respect to goods of the kind, the dealer also would have made an implied warranty of merchantability.

The elements of an implied warranty of fitness for a particular purpose differ from an implied warranty of merchantability in three significant ways. First, the seller need not be a merchant. Section 2-315 applies to all sellers whether merchants or non-merchants. Second, the buyer must prove that the seller had reason to know of the use for which the buyer purchased the goods and that the buyer was relying on the seller's judgment or skill when purchasing the goods. Third, the buyer must prove actual reliance on the seller's assurances or acts.

EXAMPLE **8:** Suppose that in Example 7, the buyer walked into the dealer's store and purchased hydraulic fluid with no advice from the dealer and without consulting any person. Because the buyer did not rely on the dealer's skill or knowledge to select suitable fluid, the dealer did not make a warranty of fitness for a particular purpose. If the dealer were a merchant with respect to goods of that kind, however, the dealer would have made an implied warranty of merchantability.

Courts first look to the parties' relative knowledge and sophistication to determine whether § 2-315 claims have merit, but they also will consider whether the buyer insisted on a particular brand, made written or oral expressions of reliance, or initiated the transaction.

Implicit in § 2-315 is the idea that "particular" means something other than that which is normal. Were this otherwise, buyers would regularly assert that they purchased goods for the particular purpose of deriving all ordinary uses and benefits one might normally expect from the goods. To recognize this assertion as a valid § 2-315 claim would undermine the section's narrow scope and frustrate the clear intent of the section. Official Comment 2 to § 2-315 recognizes the difference between an ordinary and a particular purpose:

A "particular purpose" differs from the ordinary purpose for which the goods are used in that it envisages a specific use by the buyer which is peculiar to the nature of his business whereas the ordinary purposes for which goods are used are those envisaged in the concept of merchantability and go to uses which are customarily made of the goods in question. For example, shoes are generally used for the purpose of walking upon ordinary ground, but a seller may know that a particular pair was selected to be used for climbing mountains.

E. WARRANTIES OF TITLE AND AGAINST INFRINGEMENT

Revised § 2-312 provides for the creation of warranties of title and against infringement. The essence of a sales transaction is the "passing of title from the seller to the buyer for a price." § 2-106(1). Sellers warrant, as a matter of law, that title to the goods they convey shall be good and that the conveyance is rightful. Rev. § 2-312(1)(a). This warranty also assures that title to the goods shall be free of all possessory or security interests, liens, and encumbrances, except for those of which the buyer is aware at the time of sale. Rev. § 2-312(1)(b). The 2003 amendments to Article 2 broaden the scope of the warranty of title by providing that not only must the title be good and the transfer rightful, but also that the transfer must not "unreasonably expose the buyer to litigation because of any colorable claim to or interest in the goods." Rev. § 2-312(1)(a). This concept was taken from the comments to former Article 2, and it is in accord with the cases that have addressed this issue.

Revised § 2-312(2) provides that a merchant regularly dealing in goods of the kind sold warrants that the goods will be free of a third party's claim of infringement. A claim of infringement may arise, for example, if the seller sells goods that are subject to a patent or a trademark and the seller does not have a patent or trademark license to sell such goods. If a seller provides goods in compliance with specifications drawn by the buyer, however, the seller makes no implied warranty against infringement and the buyer must indemnify the seller against loss in the event that the buyer's specifications cause the seller to violate the trademark or patent rights of third parties. Rev. § 2-312(2).

Unlike the prior law, revised Article 2 allows the seller to disclaim not only the warranty of title but also the warranty against infringement. Rev. § 2-312(3). The seller can disclaim the warranty of title or the warranty of noninfringement under this section by express language or by circumstances that give the buyer reason to know that the seller is not making the warranty. Rev. § 2-312(3).

F. WARRANTY MODIFICATIONS AND DISCLAIMERS

The warranty provisions are based on the presumption that in a contract for sale the risk of product defectiveness is and should be on the seller. This presumption is tempered, however, by the policy of freedom of contract that underlies Article 2. Thus, Rev. § 2-316 acknowledges that the parties may modify or disclaim express and implied warranties made under Rev. §§ 2-313, 2-314, and 2-315 during the bargaining process. This section establishes guidelines to be used to determine whether a warranty modification or disclaimer will be effective. Revised § 2-312 contains its own provision on disclaiming the implied warranty of title and noninfringement.

Effective warranty disclaimers do more than limit the remedies available to buyers. They may remove all basis for a remedy. Because of this, many courts have shown a disfavor for disclaimers and have developed a tendency to resolve doubts in favor of buyers.

1. DISCLAIMER OF EXPRESS WARRANTIES

When reviewing the validity of a disclaimer of an express warranty, all statements and conduct of the parties that relate to both the creation and the negation of the express warranty must be considered. Rev. § 2-316(1). These terms and acts are to be construed as consistent with each other whenever it is reasonable to do so. *Id.* Where unreasonable, the disclaimer will not be given effect. *Id.* The evidence that one can use to establish both the creation and negation of the express warranty is subject to the parol evidence rule discussed in Chapter 3. If the seller's assurances or descriptions created an express warranty under the test of Rev. § 2-313 discussed previously, the next issue is whether those representations are part of the contract given the operation of the parol evidence rule. If the representations are part of the contract, no effect will be given to disclaimers inconsistent with the express warranty. If the representations are not part of the contract, then the disclaimer of the express warranty will be effective as it is not inconsistent with any other term of the contract.

- -

EXAMPLE 9: A buyer purchased a washing machine from a dealer. The dealer expressly warranted the machine was merchantable. The dealer's express warranty of merchantability might not be inconsistent with a disclaimer that refutes any guarantee that the machine tub will spin at 100 revolutions per minute (rpm). This disclaimer will remain effective. But the same express warranty would be inconsistent with a disclaimer that refutes a guarantee that the machine will clean clothes. The latter disclaimer will not be effective.

EXAMPLE 10: Assume, in Example 9, that the dealer orally represented that the washing machine tub would spin at 100 rpm. The buyer and the dealer then signed a document purporting to be totally integrated. The document contained a disclaimer of all express warranties. If the oral representation is excluded from evidence because of the parol evidence rule, then the disclaimer is not inconsistent with the express warranty because the warranty is not part of the contract. Therefore the disclaimer would be effective.

- -

2. DISCLAIMER OF IMPLIED WARRANTIES OF MERCHANTABILITY AND FITNESS FOR A PARTICULAR PURPOSE

Subsections (2) and (3) of Rev. § 2-316 regulate modifications and disclaimers of implied warranties of merchantability and fitness for a particular purpose. These subsections govern warranty modifications and disclaimers that are part of the contract at formation as well as those that occur after sale under Rev. § 2-209. The general principles governing warranty modifications and disclaimers of implied warranties of merchantability and fitness for a particular purpose are in subsection (2) of Rev. § 2-316. Subsection (3) operates as a specialized exception to subsection (2) principles.

Under former Article 2, any written disclaimer of implied warranties either of merchantability or fitness for a particular purpose had to be "conspicuous." Former § 2-316(2). "Conspicuous" was defined as language "so written that a reasonable person against whom it is to operate ought to have noticed it." Former § 1-201(10). Under this standard, conspicuousness could be determined by such factors as print size and color in relation to the rest of the document; the use of italicized, underscored, indented, bold, or capitalized print; the print's location on the document; and the parties' relative sophistication.

Also under former Article 2, a disclaimer of the implied warranty of merchantability need not have been in writing, but if the disclaimer was in writing, the disclaimer must have been conspicuous. Whether the disclaimer was oral or written, it must have mentioned the word "merchantability" so that the buyer knew the seller was disclaiming or modifying the warranty of merchantability. Former § 2-316(2). An example of a disclaimer under these rules would be a written document that provides in all capital letters, in contrast to the rest of the document which is in normal type: "THE SELLER DISCLAIMS ANY IMPLIED WARRANTY OF MERCHANTABILITY."

Former § 2-316(2) also governed disclaimers of the implied warranty of fitness for a particular purpose. These disclaimers had to be both written and conspicuous. However, the disclaimer need not have made specific reference to the term "fitness for a particular purpose." General language of disclaimer generally would effectively negate this warranty. An example of a disclaimer of the implied warranty of fitness was given in the statute with the requirement that the language be conspicuous: "There are no warranties which extend beyond the descriptions on the face hereof."

The 2003 amendments make one change to the above described rules in relation to warranty disclaimers or modification in nonconsumer contracts and make two changes to former § 2-316(2) for disclaimers of implied warranties in consumer contracts. In a nonconsumer contract, the disclaimer may be in a "record" instead of a "writing." In consumer contracts, to disclaim the implied warranty of merchantability, the disclaimer must be in a record, be conspicuous, and use the following language: "the seller undertakes no responsibility for the quality of the goods except as otherwise provided in this contract." Rev. § 2-316(2). To disclaim the implied warranty of fitness in a consumer contract, the disclaimer must be in a record, be conspicuous, and use the following language: "the seller assumes no responsibility that the goods will be fit for any particular purpose for which you may be buying these goods, except as otherwise provided in the contract." Rev. § 2-316(2). The required language sufficient in a consumer contract to disclaim the implied warranty of merchantability and the implied warranty of fitness for a particular purpose will also be sufficient in a nonconsumer contract. Rev. § 2-316(2).

Exceptions. Revised § 2-316(3) establishes several exceptions to the requirements of Rev. § 2-316(2). First, sellers may disclaim implied warranties by incorporating the conditional terms "as is," "with all faults," or other language that "in common understanding calls the buyer's attention to the exclusion of warranties and makes plain that there is no implied warranty." Rev. § 2-316(3)(a). Although former § 2-316(3)(a), unlike former § 2-316(2), did not require conspicuousness, some courts have extended the requirement of conspicuousness to language used under former § 2-316(3)(a) to attempt to avoid the problem of unfair surprise to the buyer. Under the 2003 amendments, if the disclaimer of implied warranties in a consumer contract is through an "as is" or "with all faults" provision, that language must be conspicuously set forth in a record if the consumer contract is evidenced by a record. Rev. § 2-316(3).

Implied warranties may also be disclaimed when the buyer voluntarily examines the goods prior to the sale. Rev. § 2-316(3)(b). The section states that no implied warranty will extend to defects that could have reasonably been discovered during this examination. The former Official Comments expanded this protection for sellers by suggesting that the risk of defect should shift to the buyer simply upon the seller's demand that the buyer examine the goods. Under the 2003 amendments, this comment language has now been moved into the statutory text of Rev. § 2-316(3)(b) so that upon such a demand by the seller, the buyer is put on notice that the buyer now bears the burden of finding all discoverable defects in the goods.

Finally, sellers may be able to disclaim implied warranties by relying on course of dealing, course of performance, or usage of trade. Rev. § 2-316(3)(c). This provision allows courts to give effect to disclaimer clauses that do not meet the formal requirements of Rev. § 2-316 when parties to the transaction are at arm's length, are equipped with equivalent knowledge, and have evidenced an intent to be bound by the disclaimer through the totality of their conduct leading up to the sale. Courts were most willing to use former § 2-316(3)(c) to resolve disputes involving parties who have used and honored similar disclaimers in prior transactions.

EXAMPLE 11: A contractor purchased scaffold planking from a tool supplier. The sales contract contained the same small, inconspicuous disclaimer of the implied warranty of merchantability that had appeared on previous contracts between the contractor and the supplier during a fifteen-year period. On several prior occasions, the supplier had refused to replace defective portions of scaffolding, relying on the disclaimer. The contractor never objected to the supplier's practice. The planking collapsed and injured one of the contractor's employees. The course of dealings alone would not result in a disclaimer of the implied warranty because the disclaimer was not conspicuous. However, the course of dealings could validate the written disclaimer because the contractor's knowledge of the disclaimer may have rendered the writing conspicuous for the contractor.

----

3. DISCLAIMER OF WARRANTIES OF TITLE AND AGAINST INFRINGEMENT

The requirements for modifications or disclaimers of the warranty of title and warranty against infringements are distinct from those related to other warranties. Revised § 2-312(3) provides that the warranty of title can be disclaimed by specific language or by "circumstances that give the buyer reason to know that the seller does not claim title, that the seller is purporting to sell only the right or title as the seller or a third person may have, or that the seller is selling subject to any claims of infringement or the like." The disclaimer by specific language does not require that the language be in a record or conspicuous. The simple recitation of a statement such as, "seller does not warrant title in the goods," when made during the bargaining process, will usually disclaim the warranty of title.

> **EXAMPLE 12:** A sheriff held an auction of goods seized upon executing a judgment. No warranty of title would exist as the circumstances indicated that the sheriff was only purporting to sell whatever right or title the creditor was entitled to sell under other state law. In contrast, if the auction was part of an Article 9 foreclosure of a security interest, the secured party would make a warranty of title unless the secured party disclaims the warranty. Rev. § 9-610; Rev. § 2-312, Official Comment 6.

G. THIRD-PARTY BENEFICIARIES OF WARRANTIES AND OBLIGATIONS

Historically, only buyers in privity of contract with sellers were allowed to recover under warranty suits. Though the strict requirement of privity generally has been abolished, the scope of the abolition varies by jurisdiction. Thus, privity still plays a role in warranty law, but the degree to which it does so is unresolved. At the time Article 2 originally was drafted, a consensus could not be found for the extension of warranties to third parties, and consequently, the governing provision, former § 2-318, provided the states with a choice of three options.

The 2003 amendments to § 2-318 retain those three alternatives for extension of express and implied warranties and revise them to also allow the seller's remedial promise under Rev. § 2-313 and the seller's obligations under Rev. §§ 2-313A and 2-313B to be extended to the class of persons designated in the three alternatives. Thus, if the seller has made a remedial promise under Rev. § 2-313 or has an obligation to a remote purchaser under either Rev. § 2-313A or 2-313B, that obligation is extended.

There are two types of extension of warranty liability to parties not in privity: horizontal and vertical. Extending warranties horizontally refers to giving warranty protection to nonbuyers who consume, use, or are affected by the seller's goods, including persons in the family or household of the buyer. Extending warranties vertically refers to giving warranty protection to remote buyers who buy from a seller other than the original seller who made the warranty, such as a consumer who purchases goods from a retailer who purchased the goods from a manufacturer who made the warranty. Revised § 2-318 Alternative A only extends warranty protection horizontally. Revised § 2-318 Alternatives B and C extend warranty protection both horizontally and vertically.

Three points are common to all three alternatives. First, under any of the alternatives, the plaintiff must be someone who the seller reasonably could have foreseen would be affected by the goods. Second, Rev. § 2-318 does not impair a seller's ability to disclaim warranties. Consequently, disclaimers that comply with Article 2's provisions, and are therefore effective against initial buyers, are usually effective against remote parties. Finally, Rev. § 2-318 extends warranty liability as a matter of law. Any attempt by the seller to exclude or limit the section's operation will not be given effect. Thus a seller cannot decide to make an express warranty only to its immediate buyer or limit the implied warranties only to its immediate buyer.

1. REVISED SECTION 2-318 ALTERNATIVE A

Revised § 2-318 Alternative A extends warranty protection, remedial promises, and obligations under Rev. § 2-313A or 2-313B to a relatively narrow class of nonprivity parties who suffer personal injury: natural persons who are family, household members, or guests of the seller's immediate buyer or, if a seller has an obligation under Rev. § 2-313A or 2-313B to a remote purchaser, natural persons who are family, household members, or guests of the remote purchaser. The warranty, remedial promise, or obligation is extended to people who fall into that category of people who are injured in person by breach of the warranty, remedial promise, or obligation.

EXAMPLE 13: A seller, a merchant with respect to goods of this kind, sold a lawn mower to a buyer. The implied warranty of merchantability arose in that sale. When the buyer started the mower for the first time, the blade for cutting grass flew loose, ricocheted off of the buyer's child, vaulted over the fence, bounced off of the neighbor's house, and speared the neighbor as he sat on his own patio. Assume that the loose blade breached the implied warranty of merchantability, in an Alternative A state. The buyer's child could sue the seller for breach of the warranty of merchantability as a natural person who was a member of the buyer's family and personally injured by breach of the warranty. The neighbor could not sue the seller for breach of the implied warranty of merchantability for either his personal injury or the property damage to his house as he was not a member of the buyer's household or the buyer's guest. If the manufacturer of the lawn mower incurred an obligation under either Rev. § 2-313A or 2-313B to the buyer, that obligation would be extended to the buyer's child but not the neighbor.

A few courts have construed former Official Comment 3 (which stated that former § 2-318 Alternative A is "not intended to enlarge or restrict the developing case law") to allow extension of former § 2-318 Alternative A to vertical nonprivity buyers. Other courts have taken former Official Comment 3 as an invitation to extend warranty protection for property damage as well as personal injury or to extend warranty protection to persons other than the buyer's household members or guests.

2. REVISED SECTION 2-318 ALTERNATIVE B

Revised § 2-318 Alternative B extends any express or implied warranty or remedial promise the seller made to the immediate buyer to any individual whom the seller reasonably could have foreseen would be harmed by the goods and whom suffers personal injury due to the breach of warranty or remedial promise. If the seller has an obligation to a remote purchaser under Rev. § 2-313A or 2-313B, then the obligation extends to any individual whom reasonably may have been expected to use, consume, or be affected by the goods and suffers personal injury due to a breach of the obligation. This extends warranty protection both horizontally (beyond just the members of the immediate buyer's or remote purchaser's family, household, or guests) and vertically (including transferees from the immediate buyer or remote purchaser if reasonably foreseeable).

EXAMPLE 14: If Example 13 occurred in an Alternative B state, the buyer's child would be able to sue the seller. The neighbor, if he reasonably might be expected to be affected by the breach of warranty, would also be able to sue the seller for breach of the implied warranty of merchantability for his personal injury harm but not for the harm to his house. The manufacturer of the lawn mower who incurred an obligation under either Rev. § 2-313A or 2-313B would be liable to the child and the neighbor as well for their personal injuries.

EXAMPLE 15: The manufacturer sold the lawn mower to the retailer without disclaiming the implied warranty of merchantability. The retailer then sold the lawn mower to the buyer as in Example 13. The buyer used the lawn mower and the same harm resulted as in Example 13; in addition, the buyer's person and the buyer's house were

harmed by the flying blade. In an Alternative B state, the
buyer could sue the manufacturer directly for breach of
the implied warranty of merchantability for his personal
injury but not for the harm to his house. Both the buyer's
child and the neighbor would be able to sue the manufacturer for their personal injury harm, if both persons
reasonably were expected to be affected by the breach,
but not for damage to other property such as the neighbor's house.

----

3. REVISED SECTION 2-318 ALTERNATIVE C

Revised § 2-318 Alternative C covers both vertical and horizontal nonprivity parties. It differs from Alternative B by extending
coverage to entities other than individual and by allowing recovery for all injuries—including economic loss and property damage—not just for personal injuries. Under Alternative C, a seller
cannot refuse to extend a warranty, remedial promise, or Rev. §
2-313A or 2-313B obligations for personal injury damages. The
negative implication of that provision is that a seller can limit its
liability for nonpersonal injury losses by limiting the extension
of the warranty, remedial promise, or Rev. § 2-313A or 2-313B
obligation to the extent that nonpersonal injury losses occur.[1]

EXAMPLE **16:** In Examples 13 through 15, in an Alternative C state, the buyer and the buyer's child would be able

1. There is no consensus on the scope and extent of damages allowed under
former Alternative C. Most courts have not allowed the recovery by nonprivity
parties, under this provision, for all economic injuries. For direct economic loss
(i.e. loss to the goods sold), the result often depends on the type of warranty
under which the claim is based. For breach of an express warranty, most courts
allow recovery for direct economic damages. Most courts have not allowed
recovery if the claim arises from the breach of an implied warranty, though
consumers have a better chance for recovery. The courts have rarely allowed
nonprivity parties to recover consequential economic losses (e.g., anticipated
profits).

to sue for all injuries. In addition, the neighbor could recover for his personal injury as well as for the harm to his house. The seller who made the implied warranty would be able to provide in the contract that the warranty is not extended to persons who suffer nonpersonal injury loss, and such a term would be enforceable. The manufacturer of the lawn mower would be liable for its Rev. § 2-313A or § 2-313B obligation to the remote purchaser, the remote purchaser's child and the neighbor for all harm caused by the breach.

- -

CHAPTER

FIVE

OFFER, ACCEPTANCE, AND TERMS IN THE HARD CASE: SECTION 2-207 AND THE BATTLE OF THE FORMS

A. INTRODUCTION

Prior to the Code, American courts generally followed the common law "mirror image" rule. Under this rule, any response to an offer which purported to be an acceptance but varied the terms of the offer was treated as a counteroffer. In the sales context, this common law rule led to paperwork warfare commonly referred to as the "battle of the forms."

This battle typically progressed in the following manner: (1) the seller would give a quotation outlining the terms of a proposed sale, (2) the buyer would submit a purchase order containing the buyer's terms, and (3) the seller would counter with a form invoice which again set out the seller's terms. Typically, the blanks on the seller's and buyer's forms were filled in with the same terms (e.g., price, quantity, the type of item) but the other terms on the form were not identical. Those nonidentical terms generally concerned warranties and remedies.

Under the common law rule, the terms of the last form controlled because if the party receiving the last form performed, that performance was seen as consent to those terms in the last, form. The exchange of forms itself did not result in a contract. The last form was treated as a counteroffer, and the acceptance of the counteroffer occurred by the delivery and acceptance of the goods. Whether the buyer or seller sent the last form was merely a fortuitous happening. This situation in which the last form controls the terms of the contract is referred to as the "last shot rule."

The typical battle of the forms situation takes place in a business milieu where forms are exchanged by purchasing departments and shipping departments. The forms are drafted by each party's respective legal department with an eye toward protecting each side's interests. The purchasers and sellers rarely discuss most of the terms on the forms, confining their explicit consideration of terms to just a few—usually quantity, price, and delivery. Warranties, disclaimers, remedies, and limitations on remedy usually are not discussed. Neither side typically reads the other side's form nor pays any attention to the terms contained therein unless a problem erupts with a particular transaction. That failure to discuss or read terms unless a problem exists is probably efficient, given that the vast majority of transactions proceed without any problem.

It is within this context that former § 2-207 was drafted. Former § 2-207 helped resolve both the question of whether a contract was formed as well as the question of what constituted the terms of the contract. In this context, former § 2-207 was designed to deal with three separate issues. First, given the industry practice and contract doctrine regarding offer and acceptance, when did a contract exist based upon the paperwork that the parties exchanged? Second, if a contract existed based upon an offer and acceptance in the paperwork or a confirmation of a prior agreement, what were the terms of that contract? Third, if a contract did not exist based upon an offer and acceptance in the paperwork but the parties acted as if there was a contract so that a contract was found by conduct under former § 2-204, what were the terms of that contract?

In the 2003 amendments to Article 2, § 2-207 was completely revised. This chapter will first address the issues arising under former § 2-207 as those issues set the stage for what the revisors were attempting to accomplish in Rev. § 2-207.

B. CONTRACT FORMATION UNDER FORMER SECTION 2-207

Former § 2-207(1) addressed the formation of the contract. The subsection radically departed from the mirror image rule by providing, as a default provision, that a form would operate as an acceptance even though it contained terms different from or in addition to those set out in the preceding form if the response purported to be a "definite and seasonable expression" of an acceptance of the offer or a confirmation of the agreement.

Courts typically focused on the final form's language to determine whether the form constituted an acceptance. Thus, when a final form clearly was denominated as a counteroffer or contained too many differing terms from the preceding form, making it hard to say that an acceptance of the offer had taken place, the final form was not a definite and seasonable expression of acceptance. In many cases it was difficult to tell if the form actually constituted a definite and seasonable expression of acceptance of the terms of the offer. Former § 2-207(2) contemplated that terms in the acceptance that materially altered the offer did not preclude the acceptance from being an acceptance. Some courts held, however, that if there were material terms in the responding form that were different from the terms of the offer, the responding form was not an acceptance of the terms of the offer.

One sure way to prevent a form from becoming a definite and seasonable expression of acceptance of the offer's terms was to have the acceptance form follow the language of the "unless" clause in former § 2-207(1). That is, if the acceptance form contained language to the effect that "this acceptance is expressly conditional on the (buyer's or seller's) assent to the terms and conditions herein," the form did not operate as an acceptance of the offer.

EXAMPLE 1: Crystal Inc. offered to buy 2,000 pounds of number-one grade (best quality) sugar from Sugar Beet Processing Inc. Sugar Beet's letter in response stated that Sugar Beet had no number-one grade sugar but was willing to sell Crystal 1,500 pounds of number-two grade (very good quality) sugar. Because Sugar Beet's response clearly was not a "definite expression" of acceptance of Crystal's offer, Sugar Beet's letter was a counteroffer.

EXAMPLE 2: Crystal made the same offer to Sugar Beet as in Example 1. Sugar Beet's letter in response stated that Sugar Beet was willing to sell Crystal number-one grade sugar but could supply only 1,000 pounds. Sugar Beet's letter stated that its agreement to sell sugar to Crystal expressly was conditioned on Crystal's agreement to the modified quantity term. Sugar Beet's letter also asked Crystal to "affix a signature by this clause to show your acceptance of the modified quantity term." Crystal never returned a signed copy to Sugar Beet, and Sugar Beet never shipped the sugar. Crystal later sued Sugar Beet for nondelivery. Sugar Beet's letter was not an acceptance under former § 2-207(1) because the letter made acceptance contingent on Crystal's assent to the modified quantity term.

EXAMPLE 3: Crystal made the same offer to Sugar Beet as in Examples 1 and 2. Sugar Beet responded by sending a form that accepted the offer and stated the same quantity and grade but contained an arbitration clause specifying that the parties would arbitrate any disputes. Sugar Beet accepted Crystal's offer even though Sugar Beet's form contained a term not in Crystal's offer.

Former § 2-207(3) also addressed contract formation. This section only applied when both parties sent forms to each other that did not establish a contract under former § 2-207(1) but the parties' conduct evidenced the formation of a contract. This section sets forth a specialized version of the general rule provided by former § 2-204 that the parties' conduct recognizing that a contract exists may form the basis of contractual liability.

EXAMPLE 4: Assume the same facts as Example 2 (in which Sugar Beet's letter in response stated that Sugar Beet was willing to sell Crystal number-one grade sugar but could supply only 1,000 pounds) except that after Sugar Beet sent the letter to Crystal, Sugar Beet obtained more number-one grade sugar and immediately shipped 2,000 pounds to Crystal, who accepted the delivery. No further writings were sent by either party. One day later, Crystal lost its contract to supply Mom's Cookies Inc. with 10,000 sugar cookies. Crystal asserted that no contract was formed with Sugar Beet because the writings were insufficient to form a contract under former § 2-207(1). Nonetheless, the conduct of both parties in delivering and accepting the goods provides a sufficient basis for contract formation under former § 2-207(3).

C. CONTRACT TERMS UNDER FORMER SECTION 2-207

If a contract was formed under former § 2-207(1) as described in section B above, then former § 2-207(2) helped to determine the terms of the contract. If a contract was not formed under subsection (1) but was formed by conduct under subsection (3), then subsection (3) determined the terms of the contract. Thus, in order to determine the terms of the contract, one had to determine how the contract was formed.

Former § 2-207(2) governed terms of the contract formed under subsection (1) and drew a distinction between a contract between merchants and a contract not between merchants. If a contract formed under former § 2-207(1) involved at least one nonmerchant, the contract's terms were comprised of the terms of the offer. Those are the terms that were "definitely and season-ably" accepted. The additional terms in the acceptance or con-firmation that varied from the offer were merely proposals for addition to the contract that may or may have been accepted by the other party and did not become part of the contract unless accepted by the offeror. Former § 2-207(2).

- -

EXAMPLE 5: Sam sent an appliance retailer a written offer to buy a new laundry washing machine. Sam's offer spec-ified the essential price, delivery, and quality terms, but it did not mention a maximum acceptable motor (rpm) speed for the washer. The appliance retailer's written acceptance mirrored Sam's offer, except that the appli-ance retailer's writing stated that the washer's motor speed would not exceed 3,000 rpm. Sam accepted delivery of the washer but never indicated to the appliance retailer that it assented to the new term. Because Sam was not a merchant, the appliance retailer's term that provided a maximum motor speed did not become automatically part of the contract. Rather, it was a proposal for addition to the contract. The issue would then be whether Sam's actions in accepting the machine constituted assent to that additional term. On this issue neither the text nor the comments offered much help. The issue usually was resolved by resort to common law concepts of assent.

- -

Former § 2-207(2) had specific rules to determine the con-tract terms when both parties were merchants. When both par-ties were merchants, the drafters assumed that the parties should expect that the exchanged forms would contain nonmatching terms. The general rule was that additional terms in an accep-tance or confirmation automatically became part of the contract unless one of three exceptions applied. Former § 2-207(2). The three exceptions set forth in former § 2-207(2) were (1) the offer expressly forbid the alteration of the offer, (2) the new term materially altered the agreement, or (3) the merchant objected to the new terms included in the other merchant's written form. In these circumstances, the additional terms did not become part of the contract and the offeror merchant's original terms governed.

- -

EXAMPLE 6: Sam's Appliances, a household appliance dealership, sent a manufacturer, Appliance Supply, a written offer to buy 100 new laundry washing machines. Sam's offer specified the essential price, delivery, and quality terms, but it did not mention a minimum acceptable motor (rpm) speed for the washers. Appliance Supply's written acceptance mirrored Sam's offer, except that it stated that the washer motors would not exceed 3,000 rpm. Sam's accepted delivery of the washers but never indicated to Appliance Supply that it assented to the new term. Under former § 2-207(2), Appliance Supply's maximum speed term became part of the contract despite the absence of any explicit assent by Sam's, and Appliance Supply would not be in breach of the contract if the machines did not exceed 3,000 rpm. This analysis assumed that one of the three exceptions stated in former § 2-207(2) did not apply as the term about rpm did not alter the original bargain. *See* former § 2-207, Official Comment 3.

EXAMPLE 7: Assume the same facts as Example 6, except that Sam's offer stated, "Seller may only accept on these terms and no others." Appliance Supply's written acceptance mirrored Sam's offer and stated that it accepted Sam's offer, except that it stated that the washer motors would not exceed 3,000 rpm. Sam's accepted delivery of the washers but never indicated to Appliance Supply that it assented to Appliance Supply's motor speed term. Appliance Supply's maximum speed term did not become part of the contract because Sam's writing forbade alteration of or additions to the terms of the offer. Former § 2-207(2)(a).

EXAMPLE 8: Same scenario as Example 7, except that Sam's offer did not contain the statement forbidding alteration or additions. Appliance Supply's written acceptance mirrored Sam's offer, except that it stated that the washer motors would not exceed 3,000 rpm. Before Appliance Supply delivered the washers, Sam's notified Appliance Supply in writing that the motor speed term was not acceptable. Nonetheless, Appliance Supply shipped the washers and Sam's accepted the delivery. Appliance Supply's maximum speed term did not become part of the contract because Sam's timely notified Appliance Supply that it did not agree to the term. Former § 2-207(2)(c).

The merchant opposing inclusion of the new terms in the contract would also prevent that inclusion if the merchant demonstrated that the new terms materially altered the original offer that was accepted. Former § 2-207(2)(b). As the parties in a these disputes were likely to be merchants, this provision was of crucial significance because it raised frequently litigated questions about what contract terms are "material." The general consensus was that any new term that related to performance—i.e., quality, quantity, price, delivery, remedies, or warranties—was material. For example, a disclaimer of warranty or a limitation of remedy for breach of warranty was usually held to be a material alteration. In Example 6, if the rpm term was a material alteration of the contract formed by offer and acceptance, Appliance Supply's term would not be part of the contract.

Although former § 2-207(1) recognized that a contract may be formed where the competing forms contain "different" as well as "additional" terms, former § 2-207(2) addressed only those cases involving additional terms. "Different" terms were those that conflicted with or varied from a term contained in a preceding offer submitted by the other party. "Additional" terms were those that addressed some element of the contract not addressed in the preceding offer. The omission of different terms from former § 2-207(2)'s text caused much confusion.

The comments that accompanied this section did little to solve the problem. Official Comment 3 suggested that the rules in former § 2-207(2) were applicable to both additional and different terms: "[w]hether or not additional or different terms will become part of the agreement depends upon the provisions of subsection (2)." The implication was that additional and different terms were to be treated alike and would be in or out of the contract depending on the merchant status of the parties. Official Comment 3 went beyond the stated words in former § 2-207(2). However, Official Comment 6 differentiated between the two types of terms and thus contradicted Official Comment 3. Official Comment 6 suggested that different terms, by their nature, conflicted and therefore could not be assumed to have been agreed upon. Under this reading, different terms, unlike additional terms, were not considered a part of the contract.

The general consensus was that different terms in the acceptance did not become part of the contract. However, the authorities were split about which terms replaced the different terms left out of the contract. One view was that different terms, because they did not become part of the contract, did not affect the terms in preceding writings or offers with which they conflicted. Thus, the terms contained in the preceding writing remained in the contract and controlled.

Another view was that the different terms canceled out the terms in the preceding writings with which they conflicted. This result, a form of a "knock-out" rule, was derived from the presumption that the inclusion of conflicting terms in a subsequent writing constituted notice to the other party that the terms contained in the preceding writing had not been agreed to. Under this view, the different terms in both the offer and the acceptance were dropped out of the contract and Article 2's "gap-filling" provisions supplied the missing necessary terms.

EXAMPLE 9: Sam's Appliance sent Appliance Supply a written offer to buy ten new laundry washing machines.

Sam's offer specified that the machine's motor speed must exceed 3,000 rpm. Appliance Supply's written acceptance mirrored Sam's offer, except that it stated that the washer's motor speed may reach, but will not exceed, 3,000 rpm. Sam's accepted delivery of the washers but never indicated to Appliance Supply that it assented to the different term. Under one view, Appliance Supply's different term did not come into the contract and Sam's motor speed term controls. Consequently, Appliance Supply would have breached if the machines could not achieve speeds in excess of 3,000 rpm. Under the other approach, Appliance Supply's different term canceled out Sam's term, and the contract, as it is reflected in the writings, would contain no speed term. In this case, the court would look to trade usage and course of performance or dealings to supply the missing term.

Former § 2-207(3) determined the terms of the contract if the contract was formed by conduct under former § 2-207(3) and not by an offer and acceptance under former § 2-207(1). In this situation, the terms of the contract were all of the terms upon which the writings agreed and supplementary terms from Article 2. The terms that varied between the writings, whether different or additional terms, were not given effect, but were "knocked out." The agreed-upon terms that formed the core of the contract were supplemented by the "gap-filling" provisions found in Article 2.

EXAMPLE 10: Cereal Company offered to buy from Grain Processor Company 500 tons of processed wheat, "2% or less moisture content." Grain Processor Company's letter in response stated that it was willing to sell Cereal Company 500 tons of processed wheat, ".5% to 4% moisture content." Grain Processor Company's letter asked Cereal Company to sign the form with this clause to show acceptance of the modified quality term and made its acceptance expressly conditioned on Cereal Company's assent to that term. Cereal Company never returned a signed copy to Grain Processor Company and no further writings were sent by the parties. Nevertheless, Grain Processor Company shipped 500 tons of wheat with 3% moisture content, and Cereal Company accepted the delivery. After Cereal Company lost a contract with a distributor to produce 50,000 wheat cakes, Cereal Company asserted that it formed no contract with Grain Processor Company for the sale of the wheat. Because Grain Processor Company's acceptance was conditional on Cereal Company's signature on the form, the parties did not form a contract based upon the communications under former § 2-207(1). The conduct of both parties was, however, sufficient to form a contract under former § 2-207(3). Assuming that the moisture content term was the only term in Grain Processor Company's letter that varied from Cereal Company's offer, that is, all of the other terms in the communication were the same, all of those agreed terms will control. However, the moisture content terms of both writings canceled each other out, and the Code's "gap-filling rules," i.e., usage of trade and course of performance or dealings, will provide the "moisture content" term.

D. THE REVISED SECTION 2-207 ANALYSIS

After working through the above analysis of former § 2-207 and all of its complexities and uncertainties, one should be sympathetic with the idea that perhaps there is a better approach. In contrast to former § 2-207, Rev. § 2-207 is very simple on its face.

Revised § 2-207 no longer deals with the issue of contract formation. Whether a contract is formed will be determined by the analysis under Rev. § 2-204 and Rev. § 2-206. A new subsection added as Rev. § 2-206(3) provides that a record that contains

terms additional or different to the terms of an offer may be an
acceptance if it is a "definite and seasonable expression of acceptance." Thus, the analysis in Examples 1 and 3 would not change.
The response in a record must still be a definite and seasonable
expression of acceptance of the offer in order to operate as an
acceptance. If it is a definite and seasonable expression of acceptance, the presence of additional or different terms in the acceptance does not prevent the record from being an acceptance. *See*
Example 3.

A party still may prevent contract formation by making the
acceptance conditional on the other side's agreement to the additional or different terms in the acceptance. Rev. § 2-206, Official
Comment 3. Thus, the analysis in Example 2 also would hold
true under the revision. In addition, an offer also may condition
acceptance of the offer to agreement to the offeror's terms and thus
prevent contract formation based upon an exchange of records.
Rev. § 2-207, Official Comment 2. Thus, if the offeror's record
contained a term that stated a contract can be formed only on the
offeror's terms and the offeree responded with a record that contained additional or different terms from the offer and stated that
a contract can be formed only on the offeree's terms, at that point
in time no contract would exist. If the parties went ahead and
performed in spite of the statements in their respective records, a
contract could be formed based upon the conduct of the parties.
Thus the analysis in Example 4 remains the same.

Revised § 2-207 only deals with the issue of what the terms
of a contract are once a contract is formed, no matter the method
of formation. Thus, if the contract is formed through conduct,
through offer and acceptance by the exchange of records, or
through a negotiated deal in which a final agreement is represented in one document signed by both parties, Rev. § 2-207 will
determine the terms of the contract.

The terms of a contract are terms that are in the records of
both parties to the extent of the agreement of those terms, terms
to which the parties agree whether in a record or not, and terms
provided by the Code. The entire weight of the analysis under
Rev. § 2-207 will be dependent upon how to view the evidence

of agreement to terms that are not in the records of both parties. The purported goal of the section is to eliminate any advantage in sending either the first form or the last form in the normal situation in which parties exchange forms and do not pay attention to the terms on the other side's form. Rev. § 2-207, Official Comment 2. What courts will find is evidence of agreement to terms in another party's form is an open question.

CHAPTER

SIX

CONTRACT PERFORMANCE
AND BREACH

A. GENERAL OBLIGATIONS: SELLER'S TENDER AND BUYER'S PAYMENT

Once a contract is formed under Article 2, the parties are obligated to perform their contractual promises. Failure to perform constitutes a breach of contract. Each party's performance obligations are determined by the terms of the contract. Not all sales contracts are the same. Sometimes the goods will be delivered and paid for simultaneously. Some contracts provide for payment prior to delivery of the goods; others call for payment after delivery of the goods. Some contracts of sale involve voluminous written documents with all of the terms precisely spelled out. Some contracts of sale have little or no documentation. In some contracts for sale, the parties' agreement will explicitly displace the Article 2 default rules. In other contracts for sale, the Article 2 default rules will supply all of the terms of the contract.

EXAMPLE 1: A buyer purchased a hoe at a hardware store in exchange for a check for $15. The first time the buyer used the hoe to chop weeds in her garden the handle broke. The hoe that the hardware store/seller delivered to the buyer probably did not fulfill the implied warranty of merchantability. That term became part of the contract performance obligation of the seller because the seller is a merchant with respect to goods of that kind and had done nothing to disclaim the warranty. The seller breached that obligation because the hoe was not fit for its ordinary purpose. The merchantability warranty is a default rule of Article 2 that became part of the contract, as it was not disclaimed by any agreement of the parties.

The basic obligation in a contract for sale under Article 2 is for the seller to transfer and deliver the goods and the buyer to accept and pay for the goods in accordance with the contract. § 2-301. Article 2 contains various default rules associated with the seller's obligation to transfer and deliver the goods and the buyer's obligation to accept and pay for the goods. As with most of Article 2's default rules, these rules may be varied by agreement of the parties. Rev. § 1-302. The rules governing the seller's obligation to transfer and deliver the goods presume delivery at a single time and prescribe the necessary conditions of tender of delivery. Once the goods are properly delivered in some manner to the buyer, the buyer has an obligation to accept and pay for those goods if they conform to the contract. The rest of this part of the chapter will explain these concepts in more detail.

1. ONE-SHOT DELIVERY

Unless the parties agree otherwise, the presumption in Article 2 is that all of the goods called for in a contract for sale will be made in a single delivery. § 2-307. This type of contract is known as a "one-shot" contract because all of the goods will be delivered at one time.

EXAMPLE 2: A farmer contracted with her local cooperative elevator to sell 100,000 bushels of corn. The presumption is that all 100,000 bushels will be tendered in a single delivery, unless the parties agree otherwise. This agreement could be shown not only by the parties' discussion but also by usage of trade, course of performance, or course of dealing. Rev. § 1-303.

If delivery at a single time is not feasible due to the bulk of the goods, the delivery can be made in units, in a reasonable manner and time. Segmenting the delivery is not a ground for the buyer's claim for breach so long as there is no indication that the seller does not intend to complete delivery. § 2-307, Official Comment 3.

EXAMPLE 3: In Example 2, the farmer could deliver the 100,000 bushels of corn in several different deliveries if delivery all at one time was not feasible because of the capacity of the trucks available on the delivery date. Separate delivery would not be a breach of contract unless the circumstances indicated that the farmer was not going to complete delivery.

As stated above, the obligation of the seller is to tender delivery and the obligation of the buyer is to pay. Under Rev. § 2-507(1), unless otherwise agreed, tender of delivery is a condition to the buyer's duty to accept and pay for the goods. Under § 2-511(1), unless otherwise agreed, tender of payment is a condition to the seller's duty to tender and complete delivery. If the agreement does not provide otherwise, tender of delivery and tender of payment are concurrent conditions to each side's respective duty to perform. That is, tender of delivery and tender of payment will take place simultaneously.

EXAMPLE 4: A buyer and a seller agreed that the buyer will buy 100 units of paint for $10/unit. The delivery and payment terms were not discussed. Neither party breaches the contract if tender of delivery and tender of payment do not happen. If the seller tenders delivery of conforming units of paint, then the buyer must accept and pay for them or the buyer will breach the contract. If the buyer tenders payment, then the seller has a duty to tender delivery of conforming units of paint or the seller will breach the contract. If the buyer and the seller agreed that delivery of the 100 units of paint will be on May 1 with payment within thirty days, then the parties agreed that the seller's tender of delivery will precede the buyer's obligation to pay.

- -

2. TENDER OF DELIVERY: THE BASICS

Revised § 2-503 governs the seller's tender of delivery. Tender of delivery means that the seller has to make the goods available to the buyer in the manner specified in the agreement. If the agreement does not specify a manner for tender of delivery, Rev. § 2-503 provides default rules for the manner, time, and place for tender. Tender can take place in different ways depending upon how the goods will be transferred from the seller's control to the buyer's control, such as by the seller delivering the goods or shipping the goods to the buyer.

Regardless of how the goods are going to move from seller to buyer, an essential element of tender of delivery is that the goods conform to the requirements of the contract. Those requirements are determined by the parties' agreement and the default terms that are part of the parties' contract because of the way the terms are brought into the contract (as discussed in Chapters 3, 4, and 5). Conformity requires two different things: (1) the time and manner of delivery must conform to the contract terms and (2) the goods must conform to the warranties of quality made either expressly or implicitly as part of the sale. Conformity is a central concept in the sale of goods contract. Many of the rights and duties that the buyer can exercise depend upon whether or not the seller has tendered conforming goods. Tender of delivery is a condition to the buyer's duty to accept and pay for the goods, and tender of delivery depends upon the conformity of the tender and the goods to the contract. If the goods or tender of delivery do not conform to the contract requirements, buyer need not accept or pay for the goods.

If the parties have not agreed otherwise, the presumed place for delivery is the seller's place of business or residence. Rev. § 2-308(a). To make an effective tender of delivery the seller must put the conforming goods at the buyer's disposition and give the buyer reasonable notice under the circumstances to enable the buyer to take delivery. In addition, the tender must be at a reasonable hour and last for a reasonable time to enable the buyer to take possession. Rev. § 2-503(1)(a). For example, the seller could notify the buyer that the goods are ready and available for pickup at the seller's loading dock any time Monday through Friday from 8 a.m. until 5 p.m., unless the type of goods make a tender of this type unreasonable. If the seller is delivering the goods to the buyer instead of the buyer picking up the goods from the seller, the buyer has to furnish facilities that are suited to the receipt of the goods. Rev. § 2-503(1)(b).

3. TENDER OF DELIVERY: SHIPMENT AND DESTINATION CONTRACTS

Sometimes delivery of the goods to the buyer is accomplished by delivering the goods using a carrier instead of using either the buyer's or the seller's conveyance. When goods are carrier-shipped, two different types of contracts may be used: a destination contract or a shipment contract. In a destination contract, the seller has the contractual obligation to send the goods to the particular destination. Under a shipment contract, the seller ships the goods but has no contractual obligation to ensure their delivery to any particular destination. The goods are not placed on a conveyance to wander aimlessly around the world, however. A destination usually is given. Giving a destination does not make the contract a destination contract.

This distinction between shipment and destination contracts often is difficult to discern. The parties use shorthand shipping phrases that are interpreted as either a shipment contract or destination contract. When the goods are to be shipped by carrier, as with universally accepted commercial practice, the presumption in Article 2 is that the contract is going to be a shipment contract and not a destination contract. Rev. § 2-503, Official Comment 5. Because of this presumption, the parties will have to use clear language to indicate a destination contract. When a buyer orders goods from a mail order seller, for example, if there is not an agreement to the contrary, the contract for delivery will be a shipment contract even though the buyer's address is given as the destination.

A key difference between a shipment and a destination contract is the time the tender of delivery takes place and, consequently, when the tender's conformity will be measured and when the seller is considered to have completed its obligation to perform. In a shipment contract, the tender of delivery takes place and the goods must be conforming at the time that the seller puts the goods in the hands of the carrier. The seller's obligations for delivery end when the goods are put in the hands of the carrier. In a destination contract, the tender of delivery takes place and the goods must be conforming at the time the carrier puts the goods in the hands of the buyer. The seller's obligation for delivery in this instance does not end until the carrier puts the goods at the buyer's disposal. In a destination contract, the seller carries the risk that the goods may be damaged en route. In a shipment contract, the buyer carries the risk of damage to the goods en route. *See* Rev. § 2-509.

In a shipment contract, the seller has several duties under Rev. § 2-504. The seller must make a reasonable contract for carriage and notify the buyer of the shipment. In addition, the seller must deliver to the buyer any shipping documents that would be necessary for the buyer to obtain possession of the goods. These duties only apply to a shipment contract and not to a destination contract. The provisions of Rev. § 2-504 are not necessary in a destination contract due to the seller's own self-interest. In a destination contract, the seller has no obligation to make a reasonable contract for carriage, but if the goods fail to arrive, arrive late, or are defective on arrival, the seller will be in breach because the tender at the destination is not conforming to the contract.

Although former Article 2 had some statutory shipping terms, these terms have been removed in the 2003 amendments as being out of conformity with current commercial practice. As it is quite common for parties to use shipping terms from sources other than Article 2 as well as the fact that terms often are updated in practice—something hard to reflect in a commercial code—it was decided in the 2003 amendments not to update the shipping terms in Article 2 but to delete them altogether. Thus, when parties use standard shipping terms in their agreement, the meanings of the terms must be found outside Article 2. Usage of trade, course of dealing, and course of performance will be useful in determining the meanings of the shipping terms the parties use in their agreement.

4. TENDER OF DELIVERY: GOODS IN BAILEE'S POSSESSION

Goods also may be "delivered" from seller to buyer without moving the goods when the goods are in the possession of a bailee. Unless the buyer objects, the tender of delivery is accomplished by the seller either tendering a nonnegotiable document of title covering the goods (such as a warehouse receipt) to the buyer or giving a record directing the bailee to tender goods to the buyer. If the buyer objects, then the seller must tender negotiable documents that enable the buyer to get access to the goods or must obtain the bailee's acknowledgment that the buyer has a right to the goods. Rev. § 2-503(4). The primary difference between a negotiable and a nonnegotiable document of title is that in a negotiable document of title, the document represents title to the goods themselves and in a nonnegotiable document of title, the document does not represent that the holder has good title or claim to the goods. Whether a seller must obtain and tender a negotiable or nonnegotiable document of title to the buyer usually is a matter of the parties' agreement.

- -

EXAMPLE 5: A seller and a buyer agreed to a contract for sale of 10,000 toasters located in Warehouse Storage, Inc's. facility in Des Moines, Iowa. Warehouse Storage is

independent of both the buyer and the seller. The seller
can tender delivery of the toasters by giving a nonnegotiable document of title to the buyer or giving a directive
contained in a record to Warehouse Storage to tender the
toasters to the buyer. If the buyer objects to that manner
of tender, the seller must tender a negotiable document
of title or must get Warehouse Storage to acknowledge
the buyer's right to the goods.

----

5. PAYMENT FOR THE GOODS

Once the seller has tendered the goods, the buyer can pay in
any agreed manner. If the manner of payment is not agreed to,
the payment may be made in any manner that is in the ordinary
course of business. Rev. § 2-511(2). If the seller demands legal
tender, the seller has to give an extension of time necessary for the
buyer to procure it. Legal tender is currency that by government
decree must be accepted for payment of debts. This provision is
to avoid unfair surprise to the buyer if the seller unexpectedly
demands legal tender as opposed to some other manner of payment. § 2-511, Official Comment 3. If the buyer pays with an
instrument, such as a check, the buyer's right to keep the goods
is conditional on payment of the check. § 2-511(2), Rev. § 2-
507(2). The seller's rights to the goods if the check is dishonored
are discussed in Chapter 8.

Part of a seller's tender obligation is to tender goods that conform to the terms of the contract. If the seller makes a conforming tender, the buyer has an obligation to accept and pay for the
goods. If the goods are nonconforming, then the buyer is not obligated to accept or pay for the goods. The buyer's right to refuse to
pay is protected by the right to inspect the goods. The buyer can
determine whether the goods are conforming before payment if
the buyer exercises the right to inspect the goods under Rev. § 2-
513(1). Unless the parties agree otherwise, the buyer has a right,
before acceptance of the goods or payment of the price, to inspect
the goods to determine if the goods conform to the contract. The

parties may have agreed to an inspection place, method, or standard. Otherwise, the buyer may inspect the goods at a reasonable time or place and in a reasonable manner. The inspection may take place after arrival at the destination. Rev. § 2-513(1). The buyer's payment will be due after inspection of the goods. Rev. § 2-310(a) and (b).

In some contracts, the buyer has, by the terms of the contract, agreed to give up this inspection right by agreeing to pay against documents. Payment against documents involves a transaction in which a carrier or bailee issues a document of title such as a bill of lading or a warehouse receipt. If that document of title is negotiable, the buyer has to present it to the carrier or bailee to get the goods. If the document is nonnegotiable, then it is evidence of the buyer's right to obtain the goods from the carrier or bailee. If the buyer has agreed to pay against documents, the buyer must first pay for the goods in order to obtain the document of title. Regardless of whether the document is negotiable or nonnegotiable, in cases where there is a presumption of payment against documents, the buyer has to pay before inspecting the goods. Rev. § 2-513(3), Rev. § 2-310(c). That does not mean, however, that the buyer gives up the right to recover for breach if the goods do not conform to the contract. Rev. § 2-512(2). Two exceptions to that rule of "pay first, inspect later" are if the nonconformity of the goods is apparent without inspection or if the circumstances justify an injunction against honor of a letter of credit under Article 5. Rev. § 2-512(1), Rev. § 5-109. Circumstances that justify an injunction against honor generally involve fraudulent behavior on the part of the seller in addition to meeting the requirements for injunctive relief as a matter of equity principles.

B. REJECTION AND ACCEPTANCE

Once the seller has tendered delivery and the buyer has inspected the goods, if the goods are conforming, the buyer will have breached the contract if the buyer does not accept and pay for the goods. If the goods are nonconforming, the buyer has the right to either reject or accept those goods. Rev. § 2-601. When the goods are nonconforming, no matter whether the buyer rejects or accepts the goods, the seller has breached the contract and the buyer will have an action for breach of contract.

The buyer's right to reject the nonconforming tender of goods arises from what is known as the "perfect tender rule." In many ways, this is a misleading phrase because the goods do not have to be perfect to trigger the buyer's obligation to accept; rather, the goods have to conform to the contract requirements. The contract requirements are not only what the parties may have expressly agreed to but also usage of trade, course of performance, and course of dealing, as well as all of the other Article 2 principles, such as implied warranties, that become part of the contract. Rev. § 1-303, Rev. § 1-201(b)(12). In addition, a buyer must exercise its right to reject in good faith. Rev. § 1-304. Some courts have held that a buyer's rejection is not in good faith if the buyer rejects the goods for a minor defect. The real thrust of the perfect tender rule in Article 2 is to displace the usual common law contract performance rule that provides that a party must perform its own agreed contractual obligation unless the other side has materially breached its obligations. While Rev. § 2-601 does displace the so-called "material breach" rule, it does not require that the tendered goods be perfect. What is required is that the tender conform to the contract requirements and that the buyer's rejection of those tendered goods be in good faith.

To be effective, rejection must be within a reasonable time after tender or delivery of the goods, and the buyer must notify the seller timely. Rev. § 2-602(1). Timeliness will depend on such factors as the perishability of the goods, the fluctuation of market prices, and the difficulty in discovering nonconformities. Rejection must take place before the buyer has accepted the goods.

Acceptance of the goods under Article 2 does not mean taking physical possession or control of the goods. "Acceptance" is defined in Rev. § 2-606 as the buyer, after a reasonable opportunity to inspect the goods, (1) signifying to the seller that the goods are conforming or, although nonconforming, will be accepted, (2) failing to make an effective rejection, or (3) acting inconsistently with the seller's ownership of the goods.

The buyer's indication that the buyer will accept the goods may be by express words or by conduct. This conduct could be payment for the goods or the buyer's signature on the seller's standard form. Because the issue of the buyer's acceptance is a question of fact, all relevant evidence will be examined on this issue.

- -

EXAMPLE 6: A buyer contracted to buy a new car from a dealer. Prior to the agreement, the buyer took the car for a test drive. After the test drive, the buyer paid the dealer for the car and signed a form stating that the car was in an acceptable condition. As the buyer drove home, the car's transmission disassembled less than one mile from the dealership. When the buyer tried to reject the car, the dealer contended that the buyer could not reject because the buyer accepted the car. Whether the buyer has accepted the car depends upon whether the buyer has had a reasonable opportunity to inspect the car, and in this case the answer could be no.

- -

A buyer also may accept goods by failing to make an effective and seasonable rejection of the goods, regardless of the buyer's intent to reject the goods. Rev. § 2-606(1)(b). However, failure to reject does not constitute acceptance until after the buyer has had a reasonable time to inspect the goods. For example, assume the buyer inspects the goods and discovers the goods are nonconforming. The buyer intends to reject the goods but never sends any notice to the seller. After passage of a reasonable time, that failure to reject will become an acceptance.

Acceptance also occurs if the buyer acts inconsistently with the seller's ownership. Rev. § 2-606(1)(c). The specific acts that constitute acceptance under this section vary widely, but the broad principle is that acceptance occurs when the buyer treats the goods as if the buyer owns them. For example, acceptance may be found if the buyer, knowing of the defects, ostensibly rejects the goods but uses them in a manner in which the buyer would use them if the goods had been accepted. Those acts are an acceptance only if the seller wants to treat the buyer's actions as an acceptance.

> **EXAMPLE 7:** A buyer contracted to buy a new car from the dealer. As the buyer drove the new car home from the dealer, the car's transmission disassembled less than one mile from the dealership. Based on the dealer's promise that the car would be serviced and repaired immediately, the buyer agreed to allow the dealer to replace the transmission. Over a six-month period, however, the buyer returned eight times to have the transmission fixed. Finally, the buyer purported to reject the car and sued the dealer for the contract price, contending that he never accepted the car. In similar cases, some courts have found that the buyer did not accept because the buyer's continued use of the car was predicated on the dealer's assurances of a cure. Other courts have found that the buyer's extended use of the car indicated acceptance because a reasonable buyer would have rejected the car after only several repair attempts.

However, in an appropriate case, if a buyer has to continue to use goods after a rightful rejection and the use is reasonable, such as when the buyer has a need for the goods and cannot effect a proper cover, continued use of the goods does not constitute acceptance. Rev. § 2-608(4). The buyer may be obligated in such a case to pay the seller for the reasonable value of the use of the goods.

The buyer's acceptance of any part of a commercial unit constitutes acceptance of the entire commercial unit. Rev. § 2-606(2). A "commercial unit" is any unit of goods that "by commercial usage is a single whole for purposes of sale and division of which materially impairs its character or value in the market or in use." Rev. § 2-105(5). For example, a set of encyclopedias is likely to be considered a commercial unit; therefore, the acceptance of some volumes will constitute acceptance of the entire set. If the goods are delivered in multiple commercial units, the buyer may choose to accept the conforming commercial units and reject the non-conforming units.

When the buyer rejects the goods on the basis of defects that can be ascertained by a reasonable inspection, there are two situations in which the buyer should tell the seller about those defects. First, the seller should be told about those defects if the seller has the right to cure those defects and those defects could be cured. Second, if the sale is between merchants and the seller makes a request in a record for a full statement of all defects, then the buyer needs to state all of the defects on which the buyer will rely to justify the rejection and the claim that the seller has breached the contract. A failure to state the defects in these two situations precludes the buyer from relying on the unstated defects to justify the rejection. Rev. § 2-605. The 2003 amendments eliminated the penalty—for the buyer's failure to particularize the defects when required under the section—that precluded the buyer from asserting a breach of contract and obtaining damages. The 2003 amendments also extended these rules to the situation in which the buyer revokes acceptance of the goods.

In summary, when confronted with a tender of delivery, the buyer has two options—reject or accept. Once goods are accepted, rejection is no longer an option. Rev. § 2-607(2). Rejection of the goods does not preclude a later acceptance of those goods. Even though the buyer has the right to reject only when the goods are nonconforming, the buyer can effectively, although wrongfully, reject the goods by timely notifying the seller of a rejection. A buyer who effectively but wrongfully rejects has breached the contract but has not accepted the goods. Rev. § 2-703(1).

When the buyer effectively rejects the goods, the buyer has certain duties for the rejected goods in the buyer's possession. The buyer must take reasonable care of the goods for a time sufficient to allow the seller to remove them. Rev. § 2-602(2)(b). Because this duty is created from the seller's breach, all expenses borne by the buyer to maintain the goods can be recovered from the seller. § 2-715(1).

In the case of a merchant buyer, additional duties are imposed. If the seller has no agent or place of business in the buyer's market, the merchant buyer must follow any reasonable instructions received from the seller and in the absence of any instructions, if the goods are perishable or likely to decline in value, must make reasonable efforts to sell the goods on the seller's behalf. Rev. § 2-603(1). If the goods are not perishable or likely to decline in value and if instructions from the seller are not forthcoming, the buyer may store, reship, or resell the goods for the seller's account. Rev. § 2-604. This does not constitute acceptance or conversion of the goods. *Id.*

EXAMPLE 8: A produce seller bought 200 bushels of tomatoes from a vegetable wholesaler. The wholesaler shipped the tomatoes to the produce seller 1,500 miles away. The wholesaler does not have a place of business in the produce seller's market. When the tomatoes arrived at the produce seller's market, the produce seller rejected the tomatoes because they were of a different grade from those ordered. The wholesaler instructed the produce seller to sell the tomatoes for as much as the produce seller could obtain. The produce seller, instead, instructed the truck containing the tomatoes to return to the wholesaler's location. By the time they arrived, the tomatoes were unmarketable. Although the produce seller's rejection remains effective, the produce seller is liable to the wholesaler for its failure to resell the tomatoes on the wholesaler's behalf.

C. CURE

If the seller tenders nonconforming goods and the buyer has rightfully and effectively exercised the right to reject or justifiably revoked acceptance, the seller has breached the contract. One of the principal limitations of the buyer's right to pursue its remedies for breach is the seller's right to cure found in Rev. § 2-508. Revised § 2-508 provides the seller an opportunity, in certain circumstances, to cure the breach of contract that the seller has committed by making the initial nonconforming tender.

Revised § 2-508 allows for a cure of the seller's breach of contract in two circumstances: the buyer has rejected the goods or, in the case of a nonconsumer contract, has justifiably revoked acceptance under Rev. § 2-608(1)(b) based upon the inability to find the defect prior to acceptance. If the time for performance of the contract has not expired and the seller has acted in good faith, the seller may substitute conforming goods within the contract time. Rev. § 2-508(1). If the time for performance of the contract has expired and the seller has acted in good faith, the seller has a right to cure if the cure is timely and appropriate under the circumstances. Rev. § 2-508(2). The primary concern generally will be the degree of inconvenience imposed on the buyer. In both instances, the seller must seasonably notify the buyer of the seller's intention to cure. Generally, notification of the intent to cure after the buyer has arranged substitute goods would not be timely notification. In all instances, the seller's cure must be at the seller's own expense and the seller must compensate the buyer for its reasonable expenses caused by the breach and the cure.

The seller must have performed in good faith. Usually, the seller will be unaware of the nonconformity and could not reasonably have known about it. Yet, even if the seller knew of the defect, it might still be good faith on the part of the seller to expect acceptance of the goods if, for example, minor adjustments after delivery are common in the trade or the goods delivered were an upgraded version of what was ordered, which the seller expected the buyer to accept. To cure, the seller must make a delivery of conforming goods. Anything less than conforming goods is insufficient to cure the seller's breach of contract.

If the seller meets the requirements of Rev. § 2-508, the seller has a statutory right to cure. If the buyer wrongfully refuses the seller's right to cure, the buyer has breached the contract.

- -

EXAMPLE 9: A buyer purchased two new trucks for use in the buyer's delivery business with delivery on May 1. The seller delivered one truck on April 20 that had a big tear in the seat cushion, and the buyer rejected the truck. The seller had an opportunity to cure by notifying the buyer and finding a conforming truck by May 1. If the buyer refused to let the seller deliver one new truck by May 1, the buyer will have breached the contract by denying the seller the opportunity to cure. The seller delivered the second truck to the buyer on May 1, but it was not painted correctly. The buyer rejected the truck. Since the time for contract performance had expired, the seller could cure the incorrect paint job if the seller had acted in good faith and the cure was appropriate and timely under the circumstances. Any costs caused by the breach and subsequent cure would have to be borne by the seller.

D. REVOCATION OF ACCEPTANCE

Once the buyer has accepted the goods, the buyer's ability to return the goods to the seller is very limited. A buyer may revoke acceptance of the goods only if the nonconformity of the goods substantially impairs the value of the goods to the buyer and if one of two circumstances exists. First, the buyer's acceptance must have been based on the reasonable assumption that the nonconformity would be cured, but it was not. Rev. § 2-608(a)(1). Second, the buyer must not have discovered the defect at the time of acceptance and the acceptance must have been induced either by the seller or by the difficulty of discovering the nonconformity. Rev. § 2-608(1)(b).

Unlike the right to reject goods for any nonconformity (*see* Rev. § 2-601), the right to revoke acceptance arises only when the nonconformity substantially impairs the value of the goods to the buyer. Rev. § 2-608(1). Whether that value is substantially impaired depends upon the magnitude of the defect, the circumstances of the buyer, and the purpose of the contract.

EXAMPLE 10: A buyer purchased a new car from a dealer. The dealer did not disclaim the implied warranty of merchantability. As the buyer drove the car home from the dealer, it overheated after it ran for approximately fifteen minutes. Based upon the dealer's promise that the car would be repaired, the buyer kept the car. Over a six-month period, the buyer returned the car to the dealer eight times for work on the car's cooling system. Although the buyer agreed he had accepted the car, the buyer revoked acceptance because the dealer was unable to repair the car. The buyer's acceptance of the car was based upon assurance of cure and the cure did not happen. In addition, the nonconformity of the goods, an ineffective cooling system, substantially impaired the value of the car to the buyer.

Revocation must occur within a reasonable time after the buyer discovers or should have discovered the nonconformity and before there has been any substantial change in the goods that is not caused by the defect. Rev. § 2-608(2). Revocation is not effective until the buyer notifies the seller of the revocation. *Id.*

A buyer who revokes acceptance has the same rights and duties as to the goods as if the buyer had rejected the goods. Rev. § 2-608(3). Because use of goods inconsistent with the seller's ownership may constitute acceptance under Rev. § 2-606(1)(c), continued use of the goods after revoking acceptance will constitute reacceptance of the goods if the use is unreasonable under the circumstances and the seller chooses to treat the use as an acceptance. Rev. § 2-608(4)(a). However, if the circumstances are such that continued use of the goods is a reasonable alternative, the revocation remains valid, although the buyer may be responsible for the reasonable value of the use of the goods. Rev. § 2-608(4)(b).

EXAMPLE 11: A buyer bought a new car from a dealer. As the buyer drove home, the car's transmission broke down. Based on the dealer's promise that the car would be serviced and repaired immediately, the buyer agreed to allow the dealer to replace the transmission. Over a six-month period, the buyer returned six times to have the transmission fixed. The transmission was never adequately repaired. The buyer attempted to revoke acceptance but continued to use the car because she had no other means to get to work, she could not afford another car, and the dealer would not agree to the return of the vehicle. The buyer's continued use of the car may not be a reacceptance because the buyer had no reasonable choice but to continue using the car. However, the buyer may have to pay the dealer for the reasonable use of the car.

- -

E. ANTICIPATORY REPUDIATION

So far the focus has been on the seller's tender, whether the goods conform at that time, and the consequences of that conformity or nonconformity. Sometimes, however, the parties do not wait for the time of performance to indicate that they will not perform their contractual obligation. Whenever, prior to the time for that party's performance, a party indicates that it will not perform its contractual obligations, that party has committed an anticipatory repudiation. *See* Rev. § 2-610(2) for a definition of "repudiation." A repudiation of contractual obligations is a breach of contract.

If that repudiation substantially impairs the value of the contract to the aggrieved party, the aggrieved party need not wait until performance time to see if the other party performs but has some options that it can exercise before that time. Under Rev. § 2-610, the aggrieved party may suspend its own performance and, in addition, may await performance for a commercially reasonable time or may immediately resort to remedies for breach. An aggrieved seller may, instead of suspending its own performance, continue to finish goods if performance would minimize the consequences of breach or identify goods to the contract under Rev. § 2-704.

- -

EXAMPLE 12: A seller and a buyer agreed that the seller would deliver 100 specially built stereos to the buyer for $100/stereo on May 1, with payment due thirty days thereafter. On April 17, the buyer informed the seller that it would not take the stereos and that the seller should not deliver them. This is a clear repudiation by the buyer that substantially impairs the value of the contract to the seller. The seller may urge the buyer to retract the repudiation, may sue the buyer for breach of contract, or may simply wait a commercially reasonable time for the buyer to perform. The seller could suspend its performance while it pursues one of these options. Alternatively, if it would minimize the damages from breach, the seller could continue to build the stereos and seek to sell them to other buyers. *See* Rev. § 2-704 discussion in Chapter 8.

Once a party repudiates, that party can retract the repudiation unless the aggrieved party has acted in reliance on the repudiation by exercising remedies or otherwise indicating that it considers the repudiation final. Rev. § 2-611(1). Retraction may be made in any way sufficient to indicate that the repudiating party now intends to perform. Retraction also reinstates the repudiating party's rights with due allowances to the aggrieved party for delay caused by the repudiation.

EXAMPLE 13: In Example 12, assume the seller suspended its own performance and urged the buyer to retract its repudiation. If the buyer retracted the repudiation on April 30, the seller would not have to deliver on May 1 but could take a reasonable time to finish the goods without being in breach of contract.

EXAMPLE 14: In Example 12, assume the seller suspended its own performance and urged the buyer to retract its repudiation. On April 24, the seller contracted its manufacturing capability for the next two weeks to another buyer. If the buyer subsequently attempted to retract its repudiation, it would be too late because the seller had materially changed its position after the buyer's repudiation.

- -

In some circumstances, it may be hard to determine whether a repudiation has taken place. Under Rev. § 2-609, a party who has reasonable grounds for insecurity regarding the other party's performance may, by demand in a record, request adequate assurance of performance. While waiting for such assurance, if it is commercially reasonable, the insecure party may suspend its own performance. If the other party fails to provide the adequate assurance within a reasonable time not exceeding thirty days, the insecure party may treat the failure as a repudiation of the contract.

- -

EXAMPLE 15: A seller and a buyer agreed that the seller would deliver 100 specially built stereos to the buyer for $100/stereo on May 1, with payment due thirty days thereafter. Several times between April 17 and April 22, the buyer telephoned the seller to tell the seller it did not think it would be able to resell the stereos but did not clearly say it was repudiating the contract. The seller could make a demand in a record to the buyer requesting adequate assurance that the buyer would perform. If the buyer does not respond within a reasonable time, the seller may treat the failure to respond as a repudiation.

- -

If a party demands adequate assurances when it has no reasonable grounds for insecurity, a court may find that such a demand and suspension of performance may be a repudiation or may give the other party reasonable grounds for insecurity.

F. EXCUSE FROM PERFORMANCE

After parties form contracts, the circumstances under which the contracts are performed will dictate whether the transactions are successes or failures for each party. That the expected profits from performing a contractual duty may be reduced by exterior circumstances usually is one of the risks assumed in the contracting process. However, because circumstances may radically change after contract formation, Article 2 acknowledges that it may not be equitable to enforce all contractual obligations in every situation.

Three different sections govern excuse for failure to perform according to the terms of the contract. Revised § 2-614 operates to allow commercially reasonable substitutes for shipping facilities or carriers when the original facilities or carriers become unavailable. The substituted performance is not a breach of contract. Revised § 2-614 also allows substitution of means and manner of payment if the agreed means or manner fails because of domestic or foreign government regulation.

Revised § 2-613 provides for termination of contractual obligations if goods are identified when the contract is made, the contract requires for its performance those identified goods, and the goods suffer casualty before the risk of loss passes to the buyer and without either party's fault. If the goods are totally lost, the contract is terminated. If the loss is only partial, the buyer has a choice to terminate the contract or take the goods with a deduction from the price. The buyer has no cause of action against the seller for breach. In other words, the seller's delivery obligation is excused.

- -

EXAMPLE 16: A seller and a buyer agreed that the buyer would purchase two handmade rocking chairs for the buyer's daughters. The buyer picked out two unique chairs and left them with the seller to carve the buyer's daughters' names in the backs. That night, lightning struck the seller's workshop and it burnt to the ground. In this situation, the goods were identified when the contract was made. *See* Rev. § 2-501 discussion in Chapter 7. The contract required those identified goods, and the risk of loss had not yet passed to the buyer. The loss is total, so the seller is excused from performance. The buyer has no cause of action for breach.

- -

Revised § 2-615 permits a party to be excused from performance if it would be "impracticable" under the circumstances to enforce the contract. Impracticability arises upon the occurrence of a contingency the nonoccurrence of which was a basic assumption on which the contract was made. Rev. § 2-615. In other words, a party may be excused only in the event of an occurrence so remote that neither party could have anticipated reasonably its occurrence. If impracticability is found, then the party's nonperformance will not constitute breach.

Presumably, if the contingent event were foreseeable, the parties were in a position to protect themselves. Thus, the party who suffers from the event generally is held to have assumed the risk and may not use the doctrine of impracticability to escape performance. The courts have interpreted foreseeability as an objective test. A party will not be excused if it could have foreseen the contingency regardless of whether it actually foresaw the event. In determining whether a contingency is foreseeable, the court may look to the contract itself, including terms supplied by trade usage, as well as other factors, including the business sophistication of the parties.

Assuming an unforeseeable event occurs, a party must show that the occurrence makes performance impracticable. A term of art, "impracticable" implies that performance is either truly impossible or so commercially unreasonable as to be deemed impossible. In a few cases, for example, when a seller's factory burns down, the seller truly may be unable to perform. More often, however, the focus of impracticability inquiries rests on how commercially unreasonable it would be to demand performance.

Increased costs of performance, without some other circumstance, usually do not excuse performance. In rare, extraordinary cases, however, unforeseen price increases that alter the "essential nature of the performance" may warrant relief. Rev. § 2-615, Official Comment 4. In practice, though, courts generally have not excused sellers from contracts even after a substantial price increase.

EXAMPLE **17**: A public utility contracted with a major oil refinery to purchase from the refinery all of the utility's aviation fuel requirements. Though the market price for aviation fuel had remained stable for two decades, at the time of contract formation, the government, Congress, the · business world, and the media were debating intensely the likelihood that oil-producing countries might initiate an oil embargo. One year after contract formation, the embargo occurred and the price of aviation fuel escalated tenfold. The refinery informed the utility that it would not honor the contract. Most courts would not allow the refinery to avoid contractual liability due to the embargo-induced price escalation.

There are certain limits to the doctrine's application. For example, if a seller's capacity to perform is eliminated only partially, the seller must allocate production among its existing and other regular customers in a fair and reasonable manner and give notice of that allocation to the buyer. Rev. § 2-615(b)–(c). Moreover, the seller will not be allowed to invoke Rev. § 2-615's protection if the impracticability arises from the seller's own fault. In addition, the seller must notify the buyer seasonably if there will be a delay or nondelivery. *Id.* If a seller does not give notice, the seller may not be afforded the protection of an otherwise available impracticability defense.

Revised § 2-615, by its terms, only applies to sellers. Nonetheless, the courts generally have been willing to extend the use of the doctrine of impracticability to buyers. This view is supported by Official Comment 9 to Rev. § 2-615.

When the buyer receives notice of the seller's delay, nonperformance, or allocation under Rev. § 2-615, the buyer has some choices. The buyer may terminate the contract, which discharges the seller from any further performance obligation, or the buyer may agree to a modification of the contract as suggested by the seller's notice. Rev. § 2-616(1). If the buyer fails to modify the contract within a reasonable time after seller's notice, not to exceed thirty days, the contract is deemed terminated. Rev. § 2-616(2).

G. CHANGES IN PERFORMANCE OBLIGATION DUE TO DIFFERENT TYPES OF CONTRACTS

So far, the discussion has focused on the parties' performance obligations in a one-shot contract. Article 2 addresses at least the following three additional types of contracts: an installment contract, a sale on approval, and a sale or return. If one of these types of contracts is involved, the parties' performance obligations are slightly different from what has been discussed so far. The following discussion will focus on how performance obligations under these three types of contracts differ from those in one-shot contracts.

An installment contract is one in which the parties intend for delivery of the goods to be in separate lots and to be separately accepted. Rev. § 2-612(1). This is a contract in which the presumption of single delivery at one time is rebutted. § 2-307. In an installment contract, the buyer can reject an installment only if the nonconformity of that installment substantially impairs the value of the installment to the buyer. Thus, instead of the perfect tender rule, which is discussed in section B. of this chapter, Rev. § 2-612(2) limits the buyer's right to reject to instances of a material breach by the seller. If the nonconformity for one or more installments substantially impairs the value of the entire contract to the buyer, then the buyer can treat the nonconforming installment as a breach of the whole contract. Rev. § 2-612(3). Thus, the basic difference in the performance obligation between a one-shot contract and an installment contract is the right of the buyer to reject and the right of the buyer to declare a breach of the whole. Instead of the perfect tender rule, the "substantial impairment" rule is used to determine the buyer's rights.

A sale on approval is a sale in which the buyer is able to try out the goods for a period of time and may return the goods even if they conform to the contract. Use of the goods during the trial period is not acceptance of the goods. Rev. § 2-326, Rev. § 2-327. A sale or return is a sale in which the buyer can return the goods, even if they conform to the contract, if the buyer cannot sell the goods while the buyer has possession of them. Rev. § 2-326, Rev. § 2-327. The basic change in contractual obligation in these two types of sales is the ability of the buyer to return the goods even though the goods conform to the contract.

H. RISK OF LOSS OF THE GOODS

When goods are damaged or destroyed after contract formation but prior to complete performance by the parties, the problem is raised as to who bears the risk of loss. The party who has the risk of loss for the goods must perform its obligation under the contract even if the goods are lost or damaged; otherwise, the party will be in breach of contract. The starting point for any risk of loss question is contained in Rev. § 2-509(4): "The provisions of this section are subject to contrary agreement of the parties. . . ." The parties are thus free to allocate the risk of loss in any way that they wish, and therefore, the basic rules should be viewed as default rules that only apply when the parties have not chosen to allocate the risk otherwise.

Often the question of who bears the risk of loss is no more than the question of which party will procure the insurance against the possibility of loss, and therefore, it is best to leave to the parties this allocation of risk as they are in the best position to make the determination. Absent an express allocation of risk by the parties, Article 2 sets up a framework of rules to govern risk of loss in Rev. § 2-509 and Rev. § 2-510. Revised § 2-509 provides the risk of loss rules when neither party is in breach. Revised § 2-510 provides the risk of loss rules when there is a breach of the contract by one of the parties.

1. RISK OF LOSS WHEN NEITHER PARTY IS IN BREACH

Revised § 2-509 sets forth the risk of loss rules when neither party breached the contract prior to the occurrence of the loss. This section contemplates four transactional categories: (1) goods shipped by a carrier under a shipment contract, (2) goods shipped by a carrier under a destination contract, (3) goods held by a bailee for pickup by the buyer, and (4) other transactions not covered by the three preceding types of transactions.

A shipment contract obligates the seller to make a reasonable contract with a carrier to ship the goods and to deliver the goods to the carrier. Rev. § 2-504. In this type of contract, the risk of loss passes from the seller to the buyer when conforming goods are delivered to the carrier. Rev. § 2-509(1)(a). Consequently, the buyer bears the risk of loss while the goods are in transit.

A destination contract obligates the seller to contract with a carrier to ship the goods and to tender the goods to the buyer at the shipment destination. In this type of contract, the risk of loss passes from the seller to the buyer when conforming goods are tendered by the carrier to the buyer at the destination. Rev. § 2-509(1)(b). Consequently, the seller bears the risk of loss while the goods are in transit.

When goods are held by a bailee to be delivered without being moved, the risk of loss passes to the buyer when the buyer receives a negotiable document of title to the goods. Rev. § 2-509(2)(a). If the buyer receives a nonnegotiable document of title to the goods, the risk of loss passes to the buyer a reasonable time after the buyer receives possession or control of the nonnegotiable document of title or otherwise receives a direction in a record to deliver the goods to the buyer. Rev. § 2-509(2)(c). The reasonable time allows the buyer a chance to present the document or direction to the bailee. Rev. 2-503(4)(b). Absent a document of title, the risk of loss passes to the buyer when the bailee acknowledges to the buyer the buyer's right to the goods. Rev. § 2-509(2)(b).

If the goods are neither shipped by carrier nor in the possession of a third party, the risk of loss passes at the time the buyer receives the goods. Rev. § 2-509(3). The buyer "receives" the goods when the buyer takes physical possession of the goods. Rev. § 2-103(1)(l). Unlike former Article 2, revised Article 2 does not distinguish between merchant and nonmerchant sellers.

- -

EXAMPLE 18: A buyer signed a purchase agreement with a dealer to purchase a new car. The car was ready to be driven away, but the buyer did not want to pick up the car until the next day. The dealer agreed. The risk of loss for the car does not pass until the buyer receives the car by taking physical possession.

----

2. RISK OF LOSS WHEN A PARTY IS IN BREACH

A party's breach requires application of another set of risk of loss rules found in Rev. § 2-510. The breach need not relate to the cause of the damage to the goods.

When a tender or delivery fails to conform to the contract, the risk of loss remains on the seller until the goods have been accepted by the buyer or the nonconformity has been properly cured. Rev. § 2-510(1). This provision has significance only if the risk of loss would have otherwise passed to the buyer under Rev. § 2-509 but for the breach by the seller.

EXAMPLE **19:** Assume in a shipment (not destination) contract that the seller placed nonconforming goods in the carrier's hands and then the goods were lost while in transit. Although under the general rule of Rev. § 2-509(1) the risk of loss would be with the buyer, because of the seller's breach, the seller will have the risk of loss for the goods. Rev. § 2-510(1).

If the buyer rejects the nonconforming goods but the seller permissibly cures the defect under Rev. § 2-508, the risk of loss shifts from the seller to the buyer at the time of the cure. Rev. § 2-510(1). If the buyer accepts the nonconforming goods, the risk of loss passes from the seller to the buyer at the time of acceptance, regardless of the buyer's knowledge or later discovery of the nonconformity.

EXAMPLE **20:** Assume in Example 18 that the new car had a dent on the rear fender. The buyer took the car, but only after the dealer promised to repair the dent the next day if the buyer would bring the car back to the dealer. The buyer did not accept the car, and the risk of loss would remain on the dealer until the dealer cured the defect.

In two circumstances, the reallocation of the risk of loss to the party in breach depends upon whether the aggrieved party is insured against the loss. If the buyer accepts the goods but rightfully revokes acceptance, the risk of loss is imposed on the seller to the extent that the buyer is not insured against the loss. This risk imposed on the seller is treated as having rested on the seller from the beginning of the transaction. Rev. § 2-510(2). When the buyer, as to conforming goods identified to the contract, repudiates the agreement or is otherwise in breach before the risk of loss would pass to the buyer under Rev. § 2-509, the seller may treat the risk of loss as being on the buyer to the extent that the seller is not insured against the loss. Rev. § 2-510(3). That risk of loss will rest on the buyer for only a commercially reasonable time necessary for the seller to decide what to do with the goods.

Official Comment 3 to former § 2-510 indicated that this allocation of risk of loss is not to be disturbed by any subrogation right of an insurer. These provisions that tie risk of loss to deficiencies in the aggrieved party's insurance coverage have been roundly criticized in the commentary on risk of loss under Article 2, however, the risk allocation of former § 2-510 has been retained in the 2003 amendments.

CHAPTER

SEVEN

PROPERTY ASPECTS OF THE SALES TRANSACTIONS

The contract for sale is defined as "the passing of title [to the goods] from the seller to the buyer for a price." § 2-106(1). Even though many of the parties' rights and obligations depend upon contract law principles, there are some provisions in Article 2 dealing with the property law aspects of sales of goods transactions.

Much of the pre-Code sales law placed importance on who held title to the goods. For example, under the predecessor to Article 2, the Uniform Sales Act, it was critical to determine who held title to the goods in allocating risk of loss. Similarly, whether a buyer could sue a seller to recover withheld goods or the price of the goods also depended on who had title to the goods. Article 2 departs from this line of analysis by minimizing the significance of title. For example, the allocation of risk of loss under Rev. §§ 2-509 and 2-510 now focuses on aspects of tender, delivery, insurance, and breach, and not on whether title has passed from the seller to the buyer.

Title still plays some role in sales of goods transactions and to the extent it does, Rev. § 2-401 sets out the Code's rules concerning title to goods. The basic philosophy of Article 2 is that the location of title should not control the parties' duties to each other in the contract for sale. Rather, the terms of the contract control those obligations. The Official Comment to § 2-101 states the following:

> The arrangement of the present Article is in terms of contract for sale and the various steps of its performance. The legal consequences are stated as following directly from the contract and action taken under it without resorting to the idea of when property or title passed or was to pass as being the determining factor. The purpose is to avoid making practical issues between practical men turn upon the location of an intangible something, the passing of which no man can prove by evidence and to substitute for such abstractions proof of words and actions of a tangible character.

But that does not mean that title is irrelevant in a sales transaction. Revised § 2-401 contains the basic provision on the passing of title from the seller to the buyer to the extent that title is relevant under Article 2 or under other law.

A. TIME OF PASSAGE OF TITLE

The basic rule is that the buyer and seller may "explicitly agree" to the time and manner of title passage with three exceptions. Rev. § 2-401. First, title cannot pass to the buyer prior to identification of the goods to the contract for sale. Rev. § 2-401(1). Second, if the seller "retains title" to the goods even though the goods are shipped or otherwise delivered to the buyer, that reservation of title is limited in effect to a security interest by the seller. (That security interest is governed by Article 9.) Rev. § 2-401(1). Third, the passage of title as explicitly agreed to in the contract for sale cannot override any relevant rules from Article 9 on secured transactions. Rev. § 2-401(1).

1. IDENTIFICATION OF GOODS TO THE CONTRACT

Identification of the goods to the contract can be made in any manner and at any time to which the parties explicitly agree. Rev. § 2-501. If the parties do not have an explicit agreement on the time or manner of identification, Rev. § 2-501 contains three default rules for identifying goods to the contract. First, if the goods exist and are identified at the time the contract is made, the goods are identified to the contract when the contract is made. Rev. § 2-501(1)(a). Second, if the goods are crops to be harvested within twelve months or the next normal harvesting season or unborn livestock to be born within twelve months after the contract was formed, the crops or livestock are identified to the contract when the crops are planted or become growing crops or when the unborn young are conceived. Rev. § 2-501(1)(c). Third, if the goods are future goods (defined in Rev. § 2-105(2) as not both existing and identified at the time of contracting) and not crops or livestock as described above, the goods are identified to the contract when the goods are "shipped, marked, or otherwise designated" as referring to this contract. Rev. § 2-501(1)(b).

EXAMPLE 1: A buyer contracted with a seller to purchase a particular car parked on the seller's lot. The buyer chose this particular car after test-driving a few cars. At the time the contract was formed, the car was both existing and identified. Thus, the car was identified to the contract when the contract was formed.

EXAMPLE 2: Assume, instead, that the seller had to order from the manufacturer the car that the buyer wanted. The seller received a shipment of three cars of the same make, model, and color and then hung a tag with the buyer's name on it in one of the cars. That car is identified to the contract at the time the seller hung the tag in the car.

Upon identification, the buyer obtains both a special property interest in the goods and an insurable interest in the goods. Rev. § 2-501(1).

2. RESERVATION OF TITLE AS SECURITY INTEREST

The parties' agreement also may not alter the rule that seller's reservation of title will be treated as a security interest or the rule that the provisions of Article 9 cannot be modified by agreement. Rev. § 2-401(1). These two limitations on the parties' ability to control title passage are important because the provisions on security interests and the priority rules of Article 9 depend upon property law principles of title that parties other than the buyer and seller rely on for their rights in property. To allow the buyer and seller to alter the title rules to the detriment of third parties would undermine the system of property that operates outside of Article 2.

EXAMPLE 3: A seller sold 100 widgets to a buyer and retained title until paid. The seller delivered the widgets to the buyer. The buyer, a person in the business of selling widgets, sold 20 of the widgets to a second buyer before paying for them. The second buyer relied on the first buyer's appearance of ownership. To avoid unwinding the transaction to the detriment of the second buyer, Article 2 acknowledges that the seller has only a security interest, subject to the rules of priority in Article 9 that generally protect persons in the second buyer's position. Rev. § 9-320(a).

---

3. DEFAULT PROVISIONS

Aside from the three exceptions identified in section A.1. of this chapter, the parties may agree to the time and manner of title passage to buyer from seller. Rev. § 2-401. If the parties do not agree on a time and manner of title passage, Rev. § 2-401 contains several default rules to govern title passage. First, title passes to the buyer when the seller completes the seller's obligation to deliver the goods physically. Rev. § 2-401(2). Title passes with possession of the goods to the buyer irrespective of whether the seller retains a security interest or the documents of title are delivered at a different time or place. *Id.*

- -

EXAMPLE 4: A dealer contracted with a buyer to deliver a new laundry washing machine to the buyer's home. The dealer retained a security interest to secure payment of the price. The dealer delivered the washing machine to the buyer. Although the buyer had not paid for the washing machine and the dealer retained a security interest, the buyer had title to the washing machine when the dealer completed delivery of it.

- -

Second, when the contract requires or authorizes goods to be shipped and if the contract requires the seller to place the goods in the possession of the buyer (a "destination" contract), title passes to the buyer when tender of delivery is made at the destination. Rev. § 2-401(2)(b).

Third, if the contract requires or authorizes the seller to send the goods to buyer without requiring shipment to a particular destination (a "shipment" contract), title passes to the buyer at the time and place of shipment. Rev. § 2-401(2)(a).

- -

EXAMPLE 5: The seller, a widget maker in Peoria, contracted to ship 500 widgets to the buyer, a retailer in Orlando. The contract provided that the widgets would be sent by rail but did not require that they be delivered to any particular destination in Orlando. The buyer has title of the goods from the time the seller gives the widgets to the carrier.

- -

Fourth, if delivery of the goods is to be made without the goods being moved and if the seller is to deliver documents of title, title passes upon the delivery of the documents. If no documents of title are to be delivered, title passes at the time and place of contracting. Rev. § 2-401(3).

4. REVERSION OF TITLE

Even though the buyer may have title under the rules stated above, the title to the goods will pass back to the seller under certain circumstances. If a buyer rejects or refuses to receive or retain the goods, title passes back to the seller without regard to whether the buyer's actions were justified. If, however, the buyer revokes a prior acceptance of goods, title revests in the seller only if the revocation was justified. Rev. § 2-401(4).

B. TITLE WITH REGARD TO THIRD PARTIES' RIGHTS

The passage of title may matter for third parties' rights in the goods. The third parties' rights differ depending on whether the parties are purchasers from or creditors of the seller and buyer. Revised § 2-403 sets out the framework for dealing with disputes that commonly arise when third parties are involved.

1. PURCHASERS

Generally, purchasers of goods acquire all, but no more title than the seller either held or had power to transfer. Rev. § 2-403(1). Consequently, if a thief steals the goods, and therefore has no title at all, a buyer who purchases the goods from the thief obtains no title to them. Similarly, if a buyer believes that she bought a complete interest in goods from a seller who actually has only a sixty-percent interest in the goods, the buyer's title is limited to only that which is not held by the entity holding the remaining forty-percent interest. This concept of "derivative title" is a well-established common law principle.

EXAMPLE 6: A seller contracted to sell ten books to a first buyer. The seller then delivered the books to the first buyer. At that point, title passed to the first buyer under

Rev. § 2-401. The seller agreed to sell the same ten books to a second buyer. The seller had no title to the books or any power to transfer title to the second buyer.

In certain cases, it is possible for a buyer to obtain better title from the seller than the seller had. A seller who has "voidable," but not "void," title has the power to transfer good title to a "good faith purchaser for value." The Code does not define "voidable title," but generally the possessor of property has voidable title when the true owner intended to transfer the property but would not have had the intent had the owner known all of the facts about the purchaser and the purchaser's intent. Revised § 2-403(1) sets out four cases where a buyer obtains voidable title: (1) if the buyer deceives his seller about the buyer's identity, (2) if the seller delivered goods in exchange for the buyer's check, which is later dishonored, (3) if the buyer agreed to pay in cash but then failed to pay for the goods, and (4) if the buyer procured delivery of the goods through criminal fraud. These four situations are not exclusive, and as a general rule, any time the true owner of the property intends to transfer the ownership of the property, the transferee receives voidable title. In these situations, a good faith purchaser obtains good title if value is paid to the previous buyer who held voidable title.

Because the Code incorporates common law principles through Rev. § 1-103, common law principles may provide additional instances that would make a seller's title voidable, rather than void. For example, evidence of mistake may make a buyer's title voidable with relation to a subsequent transaction in which the buyer sells the goods involved. However, these additional instances will apply only if Rev. § 2-403 does not supplant and preempt the common law principles.

A good faith purchaser is not specifically defined in the Code. However, "good faith" means "honesty in fact and the observance of reasonable commercial standards of fair dealing." Rev. §§ 1-201(b)(20), 2-103(1)(j). A "purchaser" is one who obtains an interest in property through a voluntary transaction. Rev. § 1-201(b)(29),

(30). In general, a "buyer" may be considered a "good faith purchaser" so long as the buyer has no knowledge that another party has ownership rights to the goods in question. Consequently, a purchaser who falls within this broad definition and pays value should obtain good title from a seller who has voidable title.

EXAMPLE 7: A seller contracted to sell ten books to a buyer. The buyer gave the seller a check for the price when the seller delivered the books to the buyer. The buyer's check was dishonored. The buyer sold the ten books to a second buyer and delivered the books to the second buyer. The first buyer had voidable title. If the second buyer qualifies as a good faith purchaser, the second buyer has good title to the ten books even though the first buyer only had voidable title.

---

2. ENTRUSTING GOODS TO A MERCHANT

To protect the marketplace, Article 2 employs a special rule for sales by merchants in established commercial places. Under Article 2, any party who entrusts possession of goods to a merchant who deals in goods of that kind gives the merchant the power to transfer all rights of the entruster to a "buyer in the ordinary course of business." Rev. § 2-403(2). "Entrusting" means any delivery of possession, regardless of any conditions expressed between the parties or whether the entrusting was procured through criminal activity. Rev. § 2-403(3). A "buyer in the ordinary course" is someone who in good faith buys goods in the ordinary course who has no knowledge that the sale violates anyone else's ownership rights. Rev. § 1-201(b)(9).

The rule is based on the premise that a buyer will, and should, reasonably assume that a merchant who holds itself out to the public has good title in the goods that it sells. Thus, although the language of this rule appears to be directed to those who entrust their goods to merchants, the rule actually is intended to protect the expectations of buyers who purchase from the merchant.

EXAMPLE 8: A consumer took his home stereo to an electronics repair and resale store for repair of the stereo's broken volume control. The next day, a buyer entered the store to shop for a used stereo. The store's clerk, having repaired the stereo, had mistakenly placed the consumer's stereo with the other used stereos to be sold. The buyer purchased the consumer's stereo from the store. Two days later, the mistake was discovered and the buyer was notified of the mistake. The buyer refused to return the stereo. Because the store is a merchant who deals in the kind of goods entrusted by the consumer and the buyer appears to be a buyer in the ordinary course of the store's business, the buyer is deemed to have complete title in the stereo even though the store did not hold that same title.

3. CREDITOR'S RIGHTS

Article 2 has little to say about the rights of creditors who do not qualify as purchasers under the above principles. Generally, under non–Article 2 law, the concept of title or property interests is critical to a creditor's ability to take property to satisfy a debt. For example, if a person owes a debt to a creditor, the creditor must use a state law process, such as an execution or a garnishment, in order to seize debtor's property. The key to a creditor's ability to do so, however, is dependent not only upon compliance with the procedural rules of execution or garnishment but also upon whether the debtor has any property interests in the seized property. The passage of title to goods under Article 2 can be used to determine when the buyer has sufficient property interests in the goods in order for the goods to be subject to buyer's creditor's claims, and it can be used to determine when the seller no longer has sufficient property interests in the goods in order for the goods to be subject to seller's creditor's claims.

Revised § 2-402 addresses four issues concerning the rights of seller's creditors as against a buyer of the goods. First, a seller's unsecured creditor is subject to the buyer's rights to obtain the goods from the seller under Rev. § 2-502 or Rev. § 2-716. The buyer's rights under those sections are discussed in Chapter 8. Rev. § 2-402(1). Second, the seller's creditors may treat the sale to the buyer as void if the seller's retention of possession of the goods after the sale is fraudulent. A merchant seller retaining possession of the goods in good faith for a commercially reasonable time is not fraudulent. Rev. § 2-402(2). Third, except as provided in the entrustment rule discussed above, if the seller's creditors are an Article 9 secured party, Article 9 determines the seller's creditor's rights against the buyer. Rev. § 2-402(3)(a). Finally, except as provided in the entrustment rule discussed in section B.2. of this chapter, if the sale to the buyer is in satisfaction of a preexisting debt, the seller's creditor may have rights under other law to treat the sale as a fraudulent conveyance or a voidable preference. Rev. § 2-402(3)(b).

CHAPTER

EIGHT

REMEDIES

A. OVERVIEW

If either party fails to perform its contractual obligation, that party has breached the contract. "Breach" is not defined in Article 2. Generally, the parties' contract defines what performance is due. If that performance is not provided, there is a breach of contract.

Typical types of seller's breach of contact include repudiating the contract, failing to deliver goods, delivering goods that do not conform to the contract requirements, delivering goods in a manner contrary to that set out in the contract, or failing to perform a promise to remedy the nonconformity of the goods. *See* Rev. § 2-711. Typical types of buyer's breach include repudiating the contract, wrongfully rejecting or revoking acceptance of conforming goods, or failing to pay for the goods. *See* Rev. § 2-703. If the failure of a party to fulfill contractual obligations is not excused, then the aggrieved party has various remedies more fully set forth in Part 7 of Article 2.

The remedies for breach provided in Part 7 are specific rules designed to define the aggrieved party's expectancy interest. The aggrieved party's recovery of its expectancy interest is adopted as the primary measure of damages in Rev. § 1-305, which provides in relevant part, "The remedies provided by the Uniform Commercial Code must be liberally administered to the end that the aggrieved party may be put in as good a position as if the other party had fully performed." The aggrieved party's expectancy interest generally consists of both general damages and consequential damages. General damages (sometimes referred to as direct damages) are those damages related to the value of the goods contracted for between the parties. For example, if the seller fails to provide the goods to the buyer, the buyer could recover the difference between the contract price and the market price for those goods. That difference is the general damages the buyer has suffered from seller's nondelivery. Consequential damages are those damages related to the harm suffered as a consequence of not having the promised performance. For example, if the seller fails to provide the goods to the buyer, and the buyer was going to use the goods as components in another product, the buyer's assembly process will be disrupted by the seller's failure to deliver. Consequential damages would be the amount of harm caused by that disruption.

In addition, Article 2 allows recovery of incidental damages that an aggrieved party incurs in dealing with the consequence of a breach by the other. For example, incidental damages may be expenses in dealing with nonconforming goods, such as storage or reshipment to the seller, or expenses in finding a substitute supplier or buyer. Revised § 1-305 continues the common law policy that punitive damages may not be recovered for breach of contract unless the Code or another law so provides.

B. INSOLVENCY BASED REMEDIES

Part 7 of Article 2 contains three remedies that do not depend upon breach by a party to the contract. These remedies are triggered instead by the insolvency of the other party. These insolvency based remedies are based in part upon an idea that the insolvent party has committed a misrepresentation of intent to perform by taking delivery or payment while insolvent and that presumed fraud justifies giving the noninsolvent party a remedy to recover the goods. A party is insolvent if it is not paying its debts as they come due or is insolvent under bankruptcy laws. Rev. § 1-201(b)(23). Under current bankruptcy law, a party is insolvent if its liabilities exceed its assets. 11 U.S.C. § 101(32).

If a buyer becomes insolvent and the seller has not delivered the goods, the seller may refuse to deliver except for cash. Rev. § 2-702(1). If the goods are in transit and the seller discovers that the buyer is insolvent, the seller may stop delivery under the provisions of Rev. § 2-705. Under Rev. § 2-705, the seller has to give the carrier or bailee reasonable notification not to deliver the goods to the buyer. The notice comes too late if the buyer already has received the goods, the carrier or bailee already has acknowledged the buyer's right to the goods, or the buyer has a negotiable document covering the goods.

> **EXAMPLE 1:** A seller agreed to sell 500 cases of bolts to a buyer, with payment due ten days after receipt of the goods. The seller delivered the 500 cases of bolts to a trucking company for shipment to the buyer. The carrier issued a nonnegotiable receipt for the goods. Shortly thereafter, the seller discovered that the buyer was insolvent. The seller notified the trucking company not to deliver the goods to the buyer and told the buyer that the seller wanted cash on delivery. If the trucking company has not already delivered the goods to the buyer or has not already acknowledged to the buyer the buyer's rights to the goods, the trucking company must not deliver the goods to the buyer.

If the buyer is insolvent and already has possession of the goods and the seller has delivered the goods on credit to the buyer, the seller may be able to reclaim the goods from the buyer even though the seller no longer has any property claim to the goods under Rev. § 2-401 and has not retained a security interest in the goods under Article 9 to secure the credit. Under Rev. § 2-702(2), if the buyer receives the goods while insolvent, the seller has the right to reclaim the goods within a reasonable time after the buyer receives the goods.[1]

> **EXAMPLE 2:** Assume in Example 1 that the carrier has already delivered the goods to the buyer. Because the buyer received goods while insolvent, the seller could demand the goods be returned to the seller if the seller makes the demand within a reasonable time after the buyer received the goods.

When the seller stops delivery or when the seller reclaims goods, as described above, other creditors of the buyer or purchasers from the buyer may assert that their claim to the goods is superior to that of the seller. When the seller is reclaiming goods under Rev. § 2-702(2), Rev. § 2-702(3) provides that the seller's reclamation right is subject to buyers in the ordinary course of business or other good faith purchasers for value from the buyer. Rev. § 1-201(b)(9).

The nonconsumer buyer also has an insolvency based remedy against the seller in Rev. § 2-502. If the goods are identified to the contract, the buyer has paid all or part of the price, and the seller has become insolvent within ten days after the seller received the buyer's first installment of payment of the price, the buyer has the right to recover the goods from the seller by making and keeping a tender of the unpaid portion of the contract price. A consumer buyer is not bound by the ten-day limitation or the requirement that the seller be insolvent. Because of the many conditions on this right, Rev. § 2-502 is a very limited remedy and does not help a nonconsumer buyer whose seller becomes insolvent after the ten-day time period has run. As to those prepaying buyers, in order to secure the price already paid, the buyer must get an Article 9 security interest. Rev. § 2-502, Official Comment 2.

----

1. If the buyer files bankruptcy, 11 U.S.C. § 546(c) must be consulted to determine the status of the seller's reclamation right in bankruptcy.

EXAMPLE **3:** A seller agreed to sell 500 cases of bolts to a buyer for $5,000, with a fifty-percent payment at the time of contracting and the remaining payment upon delivery. The buyer paid the seller $2,500. The seller identified the cases of bolts to the contract. The seller became insolvent within ten days of the buyer's payment. If the buyer tenders the remaining $2,500, the buyer has the right to get the goods from the seller.

As stated in Chapter 7, the seller's unsecured creditors are subject to the buyer's rights under Rev. § 2-502. Rev. § 2-402(1).

C. SELLER'S REMEDIES FOR BREACH

If the buyer has breached the contract, the seller has several options for recovering its expectancy interest. The seller's ability to use different remedies depends upon the delivery of the goods.

If the seller has not yet delivered the goods to the buyer, the seller can stop delivery under Rev. § 2-705(1) and cancel the contract. Rev. § 2-703(2)(f). The seller will then have four options for recovering general damages: (1) resell the goods and recover the difference between the resale price and the contract price (Rev. § 2-706), (2) recover the difference between the market price and the contract price (Rev. § 2-708(1)),(3) recover the lost profit on the transaction (Rev. § 2-708(2)), or (4) recover the price when the seller is unable to resell the goods. Rev. § 2-709(1)(b).

If the seller has delivered the goods to the buyer, the seller could recover its general damages by getting the price from the buyer if (1) the buyer accepted the goods or (2) the goods were conforming and had been lost after the risk of loss passed to the buyer. Rev. § 2-709(1)(a). If the buyer has the goods and does not accept them, the seller will get the goods back because the buyer will have to reject to avoid acceptance. *See* Rev. § 2-606(1)(b). The seller also can reclaim the goods even if the buyer does not reject them if the buyer's breach was the failure to honor a check that was given for the goods, the so-called "cash sale reclamation" (Rev. §§ 2-507, 2-511(3)), or the buyer also was insolvent in a credit sale situation governed by Rev. § 2-702(2). If the seller gets the goods back, the seller then has the same four options given above for recovery of general damages. These options are catalogued in Rev. § 2-703. When choosing any of these remedies, the seller cannot recover twice for the same loss or be put in a better position than full performance of the contract. Rev. § 1-305.

In addition to general damages, the seller can recover incidental damages and, except in a consumer contract, consequential damages. Rev. § 2-710. Incidental damages are those expenses that the seller incurs in dealing with the goods after the buyer's breach. Incidental damages include costs incurred for stopping or withholding the delivery of the goods, shipping or storing the goods, and returning or reselling the goods or other damages otherwise resulting from the buyer's breach. Rev. § 2-710. Consequential damages would be the measure of the harm that the seller suffers as a consequence of not receiving the buyer's performance—not the value of the performance itself. The test for consequential damages for a seller in Rev. § 2-710(2) mirrors the test for consequential damages for a buyer in Rev. § 2-715(2).

> **EXAMPLE 4:** A seller agreed to sell 500 cases of bolts to a buyer. The buyer breached the contract by not taking delivery of the goods. The seller incurred expenses to store the bolts while arranging to sell the bolts to someone else. These expenses are incidental damages. The seller also paid interest on its operating loan for a longer period of time than planned because it did not get the contract price from the buyer when expected. That additional interest is consequential damages.

Sometimes the buyer has paid part of or all of the price to the seller and the buyer then breaches the contract and does not take the goods. As the breaching party, the buyer ordinarily would have no remedy against the seller for refund of the price. Revised

§ 2-718(2), however, allows the buyer to get a refund of the price already paid if the buyer's breach warrants the seller's refusal to deliver. That right to refund is subject to any enforceable liquidated damages clause. Rev. § 2-718(2). This right to restitution is also subject to offset by the amount of any of the seller's actual damages as calculated in Article 2. Rev. § 2-718(3).

> EXAMPLE 5: A seller agreed to sell 500 cases of bolts for $5,000 to a buyer. The buyer paid $600 when it ordered the goods. The remaining $4,400 was due on delivery. The buyer breached the contract by refusing to take delivery of the bolts. The buyer is entitled to restitution of the price paid, $600, minus the amount stated in any enforceable liquidated damages clause in the party's contract or the seller's provable damages in the absence of a liquidated damages clause.

The 2003 amendments provide a new remedy for the seller in Rev. § 2-716. The seller in an appropriate case will be able to get specific performance, including in the circumstance in which the parties have agreed to specific performance in a nonconsumer contract. However, the court may not order specific performance when the breaching party's sole remaining obligation is the payment of money. Rev. § 2-716(1).

1. SELLER'S RESALE DAMAGES: REVISED SECTION 2-706

If the buyer refuses to accept the goods contracted for, the seller may resell the goods. In Article 2, unlike under the common law rule, which preferred market price–based damages, the preferred remedy is the remedy that depends upon a substitute transaction. This substitute transaction is perceived as a more reliable indicator of the seller's harm than one based upon market price. The difference between the contract price and the resale price may put the seller in the position in which the seller would have been absent the buyer's breach. This is recognized in Rev. § 2-706, which allows a seller who resells the goods in good faith and in a commercially reasonable manner to recover the difference between the contract price with the breaching buyer and the lower resale price. If the seller resells at a higher price than the contract price, the seller need not account to the buyer for the excess. Rev. § 2-706(6). In the case of a resale, the seller also is entitled to the incidental damages and, in the case of a non-consumer contract, the consequential damages incurred as a result of the buyer's breach. Rev. § 2-710. The seller will have to subtract expenses saved as a consequence of the buyer's breach. Rev. § 2-706(1).

The resell may be either public or private, and the sale must be made in a commercially reasonable manner and must be identified as referring to the breached contract. Rev. § 2-706(2). In the case of a private sale, the seller must give the buyer notification of the intent to resell (Rev. § 2-706(3)), and when the resale is public, the seller must notify the buyer of the time and place of resale. The notice requirements for a public sale are not applied when the goods are perishable or susceptible to depreciation in value. The purpose of the notice requirement is to give the buyer the ability to protect itself from an unreasonable sale because the seller's damages will be computed based upon the resale price. A seller's failure to satisfy these requirements will bar recovery under Rev. § 2-706, and the seller's damages will be limited to those provided for in Rev. § 2-708.

EXAMPLE 6: A seller agreed to sell 500 cases of bolts to a buyer for $5,000. The buyer breached by refusing to take delivery. The seller resold the bolts by advertising in the appropriate media and notified the buyer of its intent to resell. The seller resold the bolts for $4,000. If the seller conducted a commercially reasonable resell in good faith, the seller may recover the $1,000 difference between contract price and the resale price from the buyer.

The concept of commercial reasonableness is designed to encourage sale processes that will bring a fair price for the goods.

Rev. § 2-706, Official Comment 5. Because this is a very fact-specific inquiry conducted on a case-by-case basis, some argue that the commercially reasonable standard creates too much uncertainty about what damages may be recoverable from the buyer. Others argue that the concept of commercial reasonableness is necessary to guard against unreasonable behavior in the sale process as the seller has little incentive otherwise to get a fair price for the goods. Failure to resell under Rev. § 2-706 does not bar the seller from any other remedy. In other words, the doctrine of mitigation does not require the seller to resell the goods.

2. MARKET PRICE MEASUREMENT: REVISED SECTION 2-708(1)

Sellers may recover the difference between the market value of the goods and the contract price. This is an alternative measure of damages to the contract price–resale price measurement provided for in Rev. § 2-706. The seller also may recover incidental damages and, in a nonconsumer contract, consequential damages. The seller will have to subtract from the damage amount expenses saved as a consequence of the buyer's breach. Rev. § 2-708(1).

The time of the measurement of market-price damages under Rev. § 2-708(1) varies depending on whether there is an anticipatory repudiation or another type of breach. In the case of an anticipatory repudiation, the measurement of damages is the difference between the contract price and the market price "at the expiration of a commercially reasonable time after the seller learned of the repudiation" but not later than the time of tender. If the buyer has not repudiated but has breached in some other manner, the measure of damages is the difference between the contract price and the market price at the time of tender. Obviously, the market price measure of damages only has utility when the market price of the goods is lower than the contract price. If the contract price is lower than or equals the market price, the seller will have no damages under this section.

Revised §§ 2-723 and 2-724 and normal rules of evidence govern proof of market price. The emphasis is on commercial reality that will help to approximate the harm to the aggrieved party without undue surprise to the breaching party. Thus, Rev. § 2-723(1) provides that evidence of market price at a different time and market may be reasonable in certain circumstances and subsection (2) protects the breaching party from being surprised by such evidence.

EXAMPLE 7: A seller agreed to sell 500 cases of bolts to a buyer for $5,000 under a destination contract. The buyer wrongfully rejected the goods when they arrived at the buyer's destination. The market price for these bolts at the seller's place was $4,500; whereas, the market price for these bolts in the buyer's market was $4,700. The market price will be measured at the time and place for tender that under this destination contract was the buyer's place. Thus, the seller can recover the $300 difference between $5,000 and $4,700 from the buyer.

The market price measure is an alternative measure of damages to the contract price–resell price measurement provided in Rev. § 2-706. The Code does not answer the question of whether the seller who resells at a price that is higher than market value at the time and place of tender can opt for damages under Rev. § 2-708(1). It has been argued that allowing this option violates the general Code principle that a seller should be put in no better a position than if the buyer had performed. Rev. § 1-305.

EXAMPLE 8: The seller agreed to sell 500 cases of bolts to a buyer for $5,000. The buyer refused to take delivery. At the time and place of tender, the market price was $4,000. The seller resold the goods for $4,300. If damages are measured under Rev. § 2-708(1), the seller could recover $1,000 from the buyer. If the damages are measured under Rev. § 2-706, the seller would recover $700 from the buyer. The Code does not provide an answer in this situation as to which damage measure is the correct measurement, although the principle of Rev. § 1-305 provides support for the $700 amount as the recoverable damages.

----

3. LOST PROFIT MEASURE: REVISED SECTION 2-708(2)

If the measurement of damages provided for in Rev. §§ 2-706 and 2-708(1) is inadequate to put the seller in as good a position as the buyer's performance would have, the seller may opt for the measurement of damages that would give the seller the profits the seller would have made, including reasonable overhead and incidental damages and, in a non-consumer contract, consequential damages. Rev. § 2-708(2). Both resale and market-based damages are presumed to be a better measure of the seller's harm and to be fully compensatory in most cases under the principle of Rev. § 1-305. Thus, Rev. § 2-708(2) damages only are available when the seller demonstrates that damages under Rev. §§ 2-706 and 2-708(1) are not sufficient to put the seller in the position it would have been had the contract been performed.

Revised § 2-708(2) is appropriate for three categories of sellers. First, when a buyer repudiates before a seller-manufacturer finishes production of the goods, it might be commercially unreasonable for the seller to complete production. The seller can choose not to finish production. *See* Rev. § 2-704(2). In this case, the seller will have no goods to identify to the contract nor will it have goods to resell. If there is not a market for the goods or if the market price is stable, the market price measurement would not adequately compensate the seller. Yet, the seller will have lost the profit that would have been made had the buyer not repudiated the agreement.

Second, when the seller is a middleman-jobber that never acquired the goods it intended to sell to the buyer, it will similarly have no goods to identify to the contract or to resell. In this case, the seller is barred from recovery under Rev. § 2-706 as it has no goods to resell and, if the market price is stable or hard to prove, receives nothing under Rev. § 2-708(1).

EXAMPLE **9:** A seller agreed to sell a buyer 1,000 chairs for $10,000. Before the seller started production, the buyer repudiated the contract. The seller had no chairs to resell and the market for these chairs was uncertain. If the seller can prove the amount of profit it would have made on the contract, it should be able to recover that profit from the buyer.

EXAMPLE **10:** A seller agreed to sell a buyer 1,000 chairs for $10,000. The seller planned to acquire the chairs from various manufacturers for $80 per chair. Before the seller acquired or contracted to acquire any chairs from any manufacturer, the buyer repudiated the contract with the seller. The seller had no chairs to resell and the market price for the chairs was stable. If the seller can demonstrate the lost profit, the seller should be able to recover its profit from the buyer.

Third, when the seller has resold the goods but would have made a subsequent sale of equivalent goods to the resale buyer even if the breaching buyer had accepted and paid for the resold goods, the seller is a "lost-volume seller." As a result of the buyer's breach, the seller makes only one sale when it would have made two sales if the buyer had not breached. When the market price is stable, Rev. § 2-708(1) offers these sellers no recovery and the contract-resell measurement under Rev. § 2-706 is likewise unavailing because the contract price will equal the market and resale price. Thus, a lost-volume seller receives recovery of damages for the loss of the bargain only under Rev. § 2-708(2). It is important that the lost-volume seller would have sold the goods to the new buyer without regard to the original buyer's breach and that the seller could have performed both contracts. To be entitled to the bargain of both contracts, the seller must have been able to perform both.

EXAMPLE 11: A seller sold electronics equipment at retail. The seller agreed to sell a big screen television projection system to a buyer for $3,000. The buyer repudiated the contract. The seller resold the projection system to another buyer for $3,000. Thus, the seller's resale-based damages under Rev. § 2-706 would be $0 and, because the market is stable, the seller's market price–based damages under Rev. § 2-708(1) would be $0. If the seller can prove that the second sale would have happened even if the buyer had not breached the contract, the seller could recover its lost profit on the breached transaction from the buyer.

It is uncertain whether seller's recovery is limited by Rev. § 2-708(2) to the profits the seller would have made when the measure of damages under Rev. § 2-708(1) provides for a greater recovery. Some courts have taken the position that the Code's general policy under former § 1-106 (now Rev. § 1-305)—that damages should put the seller in no better position than it would have been had the buyer performed—justified preclusion of damages under former § 2-708(1) when those damages exceeded the profits the seller would have made. Others noted, however, that former § 2-708's text and commentary contained no prohibitory language.

EXAMPLE 12: A seller agreed to sell a big screen television projection system to a buyer for $3,000. The buyer repudiated the contract because the buyer could buy the system from a different seller for $2,000. The seller had planned to custom build the system for $2,500, the cost of parts. If the seller sues for market-price damages under Rev. § 2-708(1), the seller could recover $1,000 from the buyer. The seller's lost profit on the sale is only $500. Some courts would limit the seller to the lesser lost profit recovery.

The seller may recover the profit the seller would have earned, including overhead, plus incidental and consequential damages. The language in former § 2-708(2) allowing the seller to also recover "costs incurred" less resale payments or proceeds was deleted in the 2003 amendments. Rev. § 2-708(2). "Profits" generally include the net profits that the seller would have derived from the breached contract, and "reasonable overhead" costs include a prorated portion of any fixed costs that would have been satisfied out of the proceeds of that contract. Costs incurred by the seller in preparing to perform the contract and reasonable proceeds of resale may be taken into account in an appropriate case. Rev. § 2-708, Official Comment 1. Reasonably incurred costs include monies expended by the seller prior to the buyer's breach in performance of the contract for goods or rights that lose all of their value as a result of the breach.

- -

EXAMPLE **13:** Assume a seller's cost of producing the goods is $1,000 in labor and materials and the seller's selling price is $1,200. Based upon usual production, the seller's fixed overhead that must be paid regardless of how many goods are produced is $100,000. The seller usually produces 100,000 units a year. The fixed overhead cost is $1 per unit. In addition, for this particular contract the seller purchased a particular type of coating that the buyer needed on the goods but the seller cannot otherwise use. That cost was $5. The recovery under Rev. § 2-708(2) would be $1,200 (contract price) minus costs of production ($1,000) plus the $1 in overhead allocated to this unit plus the $5 in costs that the seller spent for the coating that could not be used otherwise, for a total recovery of $206.

- -

4. RECOVERY OF THE PRICE: REVISED SECTION 2-709

The seller is entitled to recover the contract price in three situations: (1) if the buyer has accepted the goods (Rev. § 2-

709(1)(a)), (2) if the goods are lost or damaged within a commercially reasonable time after the risk of loss has passed to
the buyer (Rev. § 2-709(1)(a)), or (3) if the seller is unable
after reasonable efforts to resell goods already identified to the
contract. Rev. § 2-709(1)(b). The seller also may recover incidental damages and, in a nonconsumer contract, consequential damages.

The seller may recover the contract price of accepted goods.
Rev. § 2-709(1)(a). If the buyer attempts to revoke acceptance
wrongfully, the buyer's actions are ineffective to undo the acceptance. According to some commentators, the reason for that rule
is that at some point, the buyer should not be able to get out
of paying the price for the goods. The buyer's wrongful attempt
to revoke acceptance should not excuse the buyer from paying
the price. The seller loses the right to collect the contract price
based upon the acceptance if the buyer rightfully revokes acceptance. Rev. § 2-709, Official Comment 5. If the buyer is entitled
to revoke acceptance under Rev. § 2-608, the buyer should not
have to pay for the goods. If the goods are nonconforming and
the buyer does not revoke acceptance, the buyer may reduce the
amount of the contract price still owed by the amount the buyer
is entitled to recover because of the nonconformity. Rev. §§ 2-
714(2), 2-717.

- -

> EXAMPLE 14: A seller agreed to sell 500 cases of bolts to
> a buyer for $5,000. The seller delivered the bolts to the
> buyer. The bolts conformed to the contract requirements.
> The buyer failed to reject thus accepting the bolts. If the
> buyer fails to pay for the bolts, the seller may recover the
> price of $5,000. If the buyer attempts to revoke accep-
> tance and such attempted revocation is wrongful, the
> seller still may pursue the action for the price of $5,000.

- -

The seller also may recover the contract price if the goods are
conforming, but lost or damaged, within a reasonable time after
the risk of loss passed to the buyer. Rev. § 2-709(1)(a). The buyer

need not have accepted the goods. In this situation, the seller has performed its obligations to the buyer to deliver conforming goods and is entitled to the buyer's return performance, payment of the price.

EXAMPLE 15: A seller agreed to sell 500 cases of bolts to a buyer for $5,000 in a shipment contract. The seller delivered conforming bolts to the shipper, made a proper contract for carriage, and notified the buyer pursuant to Rev. § 2-504. Three days later, the carrier's driver lost the load in a flooded river. The risk of loss passed to the buyer upon delivery of the bolts to the carrier and the bolts conformed to the contract at that point. Because the loss occurred within a reasonable time after the risk of loss as to conforming goods passed to the buyer, the seller may recover the $5,000 price from the buyer.

In addition, the seller may recover the contract price when goods that are identified to the contract are unable to be resold after a reasonable but futile resale attempt or if the circumstances indicate that such an attempt would be futile. Rev. § 2-709(1)(b). This protects the seller if the goods are specially suited to the buyer's needs and cannot be used elsewhere. In that situation, the resale or market measure of damages is not compensatory. Should the seller actually resell the goods, the seller must credit the resale amount to any judgment obtained against the buyer. Rev. § 2-709(2).

EXAMPLE 16: The seller agreed to sell 500 cases of bolts to the buyer for $5,000. The bolts were unique for the buyer's manufacturing process and identified to the contract. The buyer repudiated the contract. The seller is unable to resell the bolts to another buyer. The seller can recover the price of $5,000 from the buyer.

----

5. IDENTIFICATION OF THE GOODS TO THE CONTRACT AFTER BREACH AND SALVAGE: REVISED SECTION 2-704

To avail itself of particular remedies in some situations, the seller may want to identify conforming goods to the contract after breach if the seller still has possession or control of the goods. Rev. § 2-704(1)(a). Identification to the contract allows the seller to take advantage of the resale provision (Rev. § 2-706) or to recover the price for goods hard to sell. Rev. § 2-709(1)(b). In addition, if the goods are unfinished, the seller may complete manufacture of the goods or stop the manufacture and sell the unfinished goods. The seller's choice in that situation must be for the purpose of minimizing harm. Rev. § 2-704(2). The buyer has the burden to demonstrate that the seller's choice is commercially unreasonable. Rev. § 2-704, Official Comment 2.

EXAMPLE 17: A seller agreed to sell 500 cases of bolts to a buyer for $5,000. The seller had an entire warehouse full of cases of bolts. The buyer repudiated the contract. The seller may identify the bolts to the contract and resell the bolts pursuant to Rev. § 2-706.

EXAMPLE 18: A seller agreed to build a yacht for a buyer for $20,000. While the seller was in the middle of building the yacht, the buyer repudiated the contract. The seller so far had spent $5,000, and it would cost another $10,000 to finish. If the seller stopped building and resold the yacht unfinished, the yacht would sell for $5,000–$6,000. In this case, the seller could recover from the buyer the contract price ($20,000) minus the resale price ($5,000–$6,000) minus the expenses saved as a consequence of not continuing to build ($10,000), for a recovery of $4,000–$5,000 from the buyer. If the seller continued building and finished the yacht, the yacht might resell for $15,000–$20,000. In this case, the seller could recover from the buyer the contract price ($20,000) minus the resale price ($15,000–$20,000), for a recovery of $0–$5,000. Either choice in this situation is likely to be commercially reasonable.

----

6. CASH SALE RECLAMATION: REVISED SECTIONS 2-507 AND 2-511

The seller has a limited right to reclaim the goods under Rev. § 2-702(2) in a credit transaction if the buyer is insolvent. Sometimes, however, the seller sells to the buyer in a transaction intended to be for cash but the transaction ends up as a credit transaction due to failure of the payment mechanism. The most common example of failure of the payment mechanism is a dishonored check. Because the buyer's right to keep the goods as against the seller is conditional on the honor of the check, Rev. § 2-507(2) provides the seller a right to recover the goods if the check is dishonored. The seller has a reasonable time under the circumstances to exercise this right. *Id.* To the extent that third parties, such as the buyer's secured creditor or purchasers from the buyer, would have an interest in the goods, Rev. § 2-507(3) would protect a buyer in the ordinary course of business or other good faith purchaser from the rights of the reclaiming cash seller. *See* Rev. § 2-403.

> EXAMPLE 19: A seller agreed to sell 500 cases of bolts to a buyer for $5,000, cash on delivery. The seller delivered the bolts to the buyer, and the buyer gave the seller a check for $5,000. When the seller attempted to cash the check, the buyer's bank dishonored the check. The seller could reclaim the bolts from the buyer. If the buyer had already resold the bolts to another buyer who qualified as a good faith purchaser, the second buyer's right to keep the bolts is superior to the seller's right to reclaim the bolts. If the sale had been for credit instead of cash, the seller's reclamation right under Rev. § 2-702(2) is available only if the buyer received the goods while insolvent.

D. BUYER'S REMEDIES FOR BREACH

If the seller has breached the contract by not delivering the goods, the buyer can either try to obtain goods that conform to the contract from the seller (Rev. § 2-716) or can recover damages based upon the seller's failure to deliver the goods. Those general damages will be measured either by the difference between the cost of the buyer's "cover" (goods purchased to substitute for those due from the seller) and the contract price (Rev. § 2-712) or by the difference between the market price and the contract price. Rev. § 2-713. In addition, if future performance is yet due from the seller, the buyer may cancel the contract. Rev. § 2-711(2)(c). If the seller has breached the contract by making a nonconforming tender of delivery, the buyer can either accept or reject the goods. If the buyer accepts the goods, the buyer can recover for the difference in value between a conforming tender and a nonconforming tender. Rev. § 2-714. If the buyer rejects the nonconforming goods or rightfully revokes acceptance of the nonconforming goods, the buyer also can recover either market price– or cover price–based general damages. The buyer also may recover its consequential and incidental damages under § 2-715.

In any event in which the buyer does not end up with the goods, the buyer can recover the amount of the price paid from the seller. Rev. § 2-711(2)(a). If the buyer has rejected or revoked acceptance and has paid all or part of the price or incurred incidental damages, the buyer may keep the goods and sell them to cover those damages. Rev. § 2-711(3). If the buyer ends up with the goods (and thus is liable for the price under Rev. § 2-709(1)(a)), the buyer may offset its damages from the price yet due. Rev. § 2-717. These various remedial options are indexed in Rev. § 2-711. As with the seller's remedies, these remedial choices are to be construed as putting the buyer in as good a position as it would have been had the seller performed and as preventing the buyer from recovering twice for the same harm. Rev. § 1-305.

1. Obtaining Possession of the Goods from the Seller: Revised Section 2-716

As previously discussed, the buyer has the ability to get the goods from the seller in certain instances of the seller's insolvency shortly after the buyer's first payment. Rev. § 2-502. In a nonconsumer case, this is a fairly limited circumstance and unrelated to the seller's breach of contract; whereas, in a consumer contract, the prepaying buyer's right to get the goods hinges on the seller's breach. Rev. § 2-502.

When the seller has breached the contract, the buyer has two additional options for obtaining the goods: specific performance and replevin. Rev. § 2-716(1), (3). The buyer may seek specific performance when the goods are "unique, or in other proper circumstances." In a nonconsumer contract, the parties' agreement to specific performance is enforceable. Rev. § 2-716(1). The drafters intended to broaden the availability of specific performance beyond the common law rule that allowed specific performance only when the legal remedy was inadequate. Specific performance often is allowed when the buyer cannot cover, and, "inability to cover is evidence of 'other proper circumstances.'" Rev. § 2-716, Official Comment 2.

- -

> EXAMPLE 20: A seller agreed to sell 500 cases of bolts to a buyer for $5,000. The seller specially manufactured the bolts for the buyer's equipment-assembly business. The seller repudiated the contract when it was able to make a contract with the buyer's major competitor for $8,000 for the 500 cases of bolts. The buyer was unable to buy any replacement bolts as no other manufacturer had the capacity to make the bolts on such short notice and in time to prevent the buyer from having to shut down its assembly operation. The buyer could seek a court order of specific performance against the seller.

- -

Revised § 2-716(3) codifies the common law action of replevin. Unlike specific performance, which arose as an action in equity, replevin always has been a legal remedy that could be had without seeking equitable relief. Thus, it is not subject to the equitable defenses or an argument of adequate remedies at law that may thwart a Rev. § 2-716(1) claim. A right of replevin arises when the buyer cannot cover, the goods are identified to the contract, and the buyer performs or tenders all contract obligations. Rev. § 2-716(3).

EXAMPLE 21: In Example 20, if the bolts had been identified to the contract, the buyer could seek a replevin order that would provide that the seller must turn over the bolts to the buyer.

---

2. BUYER'S COVER REMEDY: REVISED SECTION 2-712

If the buyer covers by obtaining replacement goods for the goods that the seller should have delivered, the buyer may recover the difference between the contract price and the higher cover price (Rev. § 2-712(2)), thereby acquiring the position the buyer would have had absent the breach. The buyer who covers also is entitled to any incidental and consequential damages caused by the breach less expenses saved as a consequence of the breach. Rev. §§ 2-712(2), 2-715. Allowing the buyer to cover and obtain cover-based damages is in line with the Code philosophy of allowing a substitute transaction as the more accurate measure of the harm to the aggrieved party.

An election not to cover does not prevent recovery of damages under alternative Code sections, but the buyer will not be able to recover consequential damages that could have been avoided had the buyer covered. Rev. §§ 2-712(3), 2-715(2)(a).

EXAMPLE 22: In January, a farmer contracted to deliver to a miller 5,000 bushels of wheat by April 30 at $10 a bushel. A March freeze killed off much of that year's harvest and drove the market price of wheat up to $15 a bushel on

April 30. The miller sought diligently to find another supplier, and on May 10, the miller covered by buying 5,000 bushels of wheat from another farmer for the then-reasonable market price of $17 a bushel. The miller should be able to recover $7 per bushel because the miller's damages are measured at the time cover was effected, not the time when delivery was to have occurred.

Cover must be accomplished in good faith. The replacement goods need not be identical to the undelivered or defective original goods so long as they are a functional equivalent. Rev. § 2-712, Official Comment 4. Buyers need not choose the least costly method of cover so long as commercially sound reasons justify the more expensive method. *Id.* The amount of damages is offset by expenses saved by the buyer as a result of the cover purchase. Rev. § 2-712(2).

EXAMPLE 23: A seller contracted to sell and ship 1,000 widgets to a buyer. The buyer agreed to pay the shipping costs of $250. Later, the seller failed to deliver the widgets and the buyer covered by purchasing them locally. The buyer's damages measured by the difference between the contract price and the cover price will be reduced by the $250 the buyer did not have to pay in shipping costs for the replacement widgets.

----

3. MARKET-PRICE DAMAGES: REVISED SECTION 2-713

Revised § 2-713 provides the measure of damages for buyers who do not or cannot replace nonconforming or undelivered goods. The buyer's damages can be measured by the difference between the contract price and the market price plus incidental and consequential damages minus expenses saved as a consequence of the seller's breach. Rev. § 2-713. Under this section, the time for measurement of the market price when the buyer seeks such damages will depend upon whether the seller repudiated the contract. If the seller repudiated, the market price is measured "at the expiration of a commercially reasonable time after the buyer learned of the repudiation" but no later than the time for tender. If the seller did not repudiate but breached the contract in some other way so that the buyer has not accepted the goods, the market price is measured at the time for tender under the terms of the agreement.

EXAMPLE 24: A seller agreed to sell 500 cases of bolts to a buyer for $5,000. The seller failed to deliver the goods. The market price at the time for tender was $7,000. The buyer can recover the $2,000 difference between the contract price and the market price at the time of tender. If the seller repudiated the contract prior to when delivery was due, the market price would be measured at the expiration of a commercially reasonable time after the buyer learned of the repudiation but no later than the time for tender.

This measure is an alternative to the contract price–cover price measure of damages in Rev. § 2-712. Because the Code does not expressly preclude a buyer from effecting cover and then seeking a higher measure of damages under Rev. § 2-713, for example, when the market price for the substitute goods drops sharply after the buyer learns of the seller's breach, it often would be advantageous for a buyer to attempt to do this. Though a few courts have allowed this, most courts, in reliance on Official Comment 5 to former § 2-713 (Official Comment 7 to Rev. § 2-713), have not permitted this, reasoning that to allow the buyer to choose market price recovery when the buyer has covered would give the buyer more then its full performance position. *See* Rev. § 1-305.

EXAMPLE 25: A seller agreed to deliver widgets to a buyer at the contract price of $50,000. The seller repudiated the agreement and failed to deliver the widgets. The time for tender was May 1, when the market price of replacement widgets was $62,000. The buyer could not cover until May 15, by which time the market price dropped to $55,000. The buyer sued the seller under Rev. § 2-713 for the $12,000 difference between the contract price and the market price at the time of tender. If the buyer prevails, the buyer will recognize a $7,000 windfall because the buyer actually was able to cover for only $5,000 more than the contract price.

The market price is measured at the place where tender would have occurred absent the breach, or in the case of rejection or revocation, at the place of arrival. Rev. § 2-713(2). This rule makes sense as the place of measurement is in the market where the buyer likely would be looking for substitute goods, making that market price a good measure of the harm the buyer suffered as a result of the seller's breach. Therefore, in a shipment contract, if the seller does not ship the goods, the market will be at the place of shipment, as that is where the seller's tender would have occurred. In a destination contract, the market will be at the place the goods are shipped to, as that is where the seller's tender would have occurred. If the buyer rejected the tendered delivery after the goods' arrival or if the buyer later revoked acceptance, market price is measured "at the place of arrival." Rev. § 2-713(2).

As to what constitutes the relevant market, it is the market for "goods of the same kind and in the same branch of trade." Rev. § 2-713, Official Comment 5. For example, if the buyer had contracted to buy goods at wholesale, the relevant market price would be the wholesale market price. Reasonable deviations are allowed for the time and the locality of measurement and to the extent that the measured goods are similar to the contracted for goods.

4. DAMAGES FOR NONCONFORMITY WHEN BUYER ACCEPTS GOODS: REVISED SECTION 2-714

Revised § 2-714 contains two different measurement rules for recovering damages for nonconformity of tender when the goods are accepted. The first subsection is a general rule that applies when the tender is nonconforming in some way that is unrelated to a warranty of quality. For example, assume the seller's tender was late but in all other respects conformed to the contract. Under subsection (1), the buyer could cover for the harm caused by late delivery. Normally, the buyer would be expected to give the seller notice of the breach, and the failure to do so will bar the buyer from using the breach as a basis of damages if the seller is prejudiced by the buyer's failure to give notice. Rev. § 2-607(3)(a).

The measurement of damages for breach of warranty for accepted goods is the difference between the value of the goods at the time and place the goods are accepted and the value of the goods had the goods been as warranted, as well as any incidental and consequential damages the buyer would be entitled to under § 2-715. Rev. § 2-714(2). The buyer also is expected to give the seller notice of this breach, and the failure to do so will bar the buyer from using the breach as a basis of damages if the seller is prejudiced by the buyer's failure to give notice. Rev. § 2-607(3)(a).

The contract price may be the best indicator of the value as warranted. In some circumstances, however, the contract price of the goods will not be an appropriate indication of the value as warranted if the seller has promised a level of quality that is beyond what is reasonable for that contract price. Resale prices obtained or appraisal testimony usually are the best indicators of the goods' value "as accepted." Damages usually are determined objectively, based on the value that a similarly situated, reasonable buyer would assign to the goods as opposed to the subjective value to the buyer. The cost to repair the defective goods may be a good indication of what it would take to measure the difference between the value as warranted and the value as accepted. In some circumstances, if the cost of repair is substantially more than the difference between the value as warranted and the value as accepted as determined by other evidence, the buyer may not be able to recover the cost of repair but may be limited to the lower measurement of harm.

EXAMPLE 26: A seller agreed to sell a computer system to a buyer to run the buyer's inventory-control software. The seller knew of the purpose and expressly warranted that the machine was capable of running the software. When the buyer received the machine, the computer crashed every time the software was run. Eventually, the seller determined that the reason the computer could not run the software was that it required a unique memory configuration. The seller had to provide some memory chips and a different operating system. The difference between the value of the goods as warranted and as accepted could be measured by the cost of providing more memory and the different operating system (what it would cost to repair the goods). Alternatively, the value of the goods as warranted could be measured by the contract price or by other evidence of what such a system that worked would cost.

----

5. CONSEQUENTIAL AND INCIDENTAL DAMAGES: SECTION 2-715

A buyer also can recover incidental damages. Incidental damages are expenses related to dealing with the goods. In addition, a buyer's incidental damages include the expenses or charges ancillary to obtaining cover or dealing with the breach. § 2-715(1). Common examples are shipping, handling, and storage fees, as well as charges or commissions related to cover purchases. These expenses must be reasonable.

Section 2-715(2) expressly provides the buyer with the ability to recover consequential damages. Consequential damages are compensation for harm to the buyer as a consequence of not having the seller's promised performance. Consequential damages can be economic loss, such as lost profits. These damages also may encompass harm to a person or to property of the buyer other than the goods. For economic loss damages, § 2-715(2)(a) codifies a form of the *Hadley v. Baxendale* test of foreseeability that is less than the "tacit understanding" test. The seller is liable for the buyer's consequential losses resulting from the buyer's general or particular needs that the seller had reason to know of at the time of contracting. In addition, for the buyer to recover those damages from the seller, the buyer had to be unable to have reasonably mitigated the loss. Finally, the loss must be proved with reasonable certainty. That requirement encompasses both a causation element and a calculation element. That is, the loss must have been caused by the seller's failure to perform and the buyer has to prove the amount of the loss with reasonable certainty. Official Comment 4 to § 2-715 rejects a "mathematical certainty" test. Thus, the consequential damage rule in § 2-715(2)(a) resembles the common law approach to consequential damages.

Section 2-715(2)(b) adopts a different rule for consequential damages for personal injury or for property other than the goods sold. All that a buyer need show as to those losses is that they were proximately caused by a breach of warranty. Instead of a *Hadley v. Baxendale* foreseeability test as to these types of losses, Article 2 substitutes a proximate cause test. Whether that is a greater or lesser standard is open to some debate.

- -

EXAMPLE 27: In Example 26, the buyer's harm due to the disruption of its business when the inventory control system did not function due to the nonconformity of the computer could be a foreseeable consequential economic loss. The buyer could recover the value of that harm from the seller.

- -

E. CHANGING THE DEFAULT REMEDIES RULES

Article 2 has two basic provisions that allow the parties to substitute other remedies for the scheme of remedies described above. The first is Rev. § 2-718(1), which allows liquidated damage clauses. The second is § 2-719, which allows the parties to agree to limit or modify remedies. Parties often agree to a liquidated damage clause or a limited remedy clause in order to specifically allocate the harm from breach of the contract. A liquidated damages clause is enforceable if it is reasonable in light of the anticipated or actual harm and, in a consumer contract, if the clause is reasonable using the additional requirements of the difficulty of proof of loss and the difficulty of obtaining an adequate remedy.

The second way that the parties can alter the Article 2 remedies is to provide for agreed remedies. The presumption is that agreed remedies are in addition to the Article 2 remedies unless the parties expressly agree that the agreed remedy is exclusive. If the agreed remedy is exclusive, it displaces the Article 2 default remedies. § 2-719(1)(b). In addition, the parties may contract that they are not liable for the other party's consequential damages. Section 2-719(3) validates such consequential damage excluders subject to the unconscionability standard. That section also provides that limitations of consequential damages in the case of personal injury when consumer goods are involved is prima facie unconscionable.

EXAMPLE 28: Assume the same facts as in Example 26, except that the buyer and the seller agreed that if the computer system did not work to run the inventory control software, the buyer's sole remedy would be to return the system for a refund. The agreement also provided that the seller would not be liable for any of the buyer's consequential or incidental damages. These generally are valid remedy limitations under § 2-719.

A recurring issue under § 2-719 is what to do about the situation when an agreed, limited, exclusive remedy is not provided as agreed or is provided but in essence leaves the aggrieved party far short of the bargained for performance. In the language of § 2-719(2), this remedy has then failed of its essential purpose. When a remedy fails, the issue is what remedies the aggrieved party then has. Of primary concern is the relationship between the agreed limited remedy and the consequential damage excluder otherwise validated under § 2-719(3). Some courts hold that when the agreed remedy is not provided, the aggrieved party can resort to all remedies for breach and the consequential damage excluder does not bar recovery of damages for consequential loss. Some courts hold just the opposite: The aggrieved party may recover damages for failing to provide the agreed remedy but may not recover consequential damages when the agreement has a consequential damage excluder allowed under § 2-719(3). The reason for the different results is the courts' perception of what the parties probably intended to happen in this situation. That is, what did the parties intend as to who should bear the consequential harm when the agreed remedy is not provided.

F. STATUTES OF LIMITATIONS: REVISED SECTION 2-725

The statute of limitations for an action arising out of Article 2 is set forth in Rev. § 2-725. The limitations period for an action for breach of contract under former Article 2 was four years after the cause of action accrued. The 2003 amendments contain the same rule but provide in addition that the limitation period also can be "one year after the breach was or should have been discovered, but no longer than five years after the right of action accrued." This accommodates the situation when the breach is discovered near to the end of the otherwise applicable four-year period. The amendments also provide that the limitation period can be reduced to not less than one year as under former Article 2 and additionally provide that the limitation period cannot be reduced in a consumer contract.

A cause of action accrues when the breach occurs, irrespective of the party's knowledge of the breach. Rev. § 2-725(2). Under former Article 2, a breach of warranty occurred when the tender of delivery was made, except where a warranty explicitly extended to future performance of the goods. When a warranty explicitly extended to future performance of the goods, the cause of action accrued, and the four-year statute of limitations began to run when the breach "is or should have been discovered."

The 2003 amendments to Article 2 provide for eight different accrual rules. The basic rule is that the cause of action for breach of contract accrues when the breach occurs. That rule is subject to the following seven exceptions:

1. A cause of action for a breach that is a repudiation accrues "at the earlier of when the aggrieved party elects to treat the repudiation as a breach or when a commercially reasonable time for awaiting performance has expired."
2. A cause of action for a breach of a remedial promise accrues when the remedial promise "is not performed when due."
3. A cause of action for which the defendant is a "person that is answerable over to the buyer for a claim asserted against the buyer" accrues when the claim was "originally asserted against the buyer."
4. A cause of action for breach of the warranty of title or non-infringement accrues when the "aggrieved party discovers or should have discovered the breach."
5. A cause of action for breach of the warranty of noninfringement may not be brought after six years after the tender of delivery to the aggrieved party.
6. A cause of action for breach of an express warranty, the warranty of merchantability, and the warranty of fitness for a particular purpose accrue upon tender of delivery to the immediate buyer and when the seller has completed any "agreed installation or assembly of the goods."
7. A cause of action for breach of the obligation under Rev. §§ 2-313A or 2-313B other than a remedial promise accrues when the remote purchaser receives the goods.

These last two accrual rules are each subject to an exception for when the express warranties or remote obligations, other than remedial promises, "explicitly extend to the future performance of the goods and discovery of the breach must await the time for performance." In that situation, the cause of action accrues when the immediate buyer or remote purchaser, as the case may be, "discovers or should have discovered the breach."

BIBLIOGRAPHY

General References

1–5 LARY LAWRENCE: ANDERSON ON THE UNIFORM COMMERCIAL CODE (3d ed. 1994 & 2003 Supp.).

3–3A HENRY DEEB GABRIEL AND WILLIAM H. HENNING, BENDER'S UNIFORM COMMERCIAL CODE SERVICE: SALES AND BULK TRANSFERS UNDER THE UNIFORM COMMERCIAL CODE (1996 & 2003 Supp).

E. ALAN FARNSWORTH, CONTRACTS (3d ed. 1999).

2–3 WILLIAM D. HAWKLAND, UNIFORM COMMERCIAL CODE SERIES (1996 & 2003 Supp.).

WILLIAM H. HENNING AND GEORGE I. WALLACH, THE LAW OF SALES UNDER THE UNIFORM COMMERCIAL CODE (rev. ed. 2002).

ROBERT A. HILLMAN, JULIAN B. MCDONNELL, STEVE H. NICKLES, COMMON LAW AND EQUITY UNDER THE UNIFORM COMMERCIAL CODE (1985).

DEBORAH L. NELSON, WILLISTON ON SALES (5th ed. 1992 & 2003 Supp.).

JAMES J. WHITE AND ROBERT S. SUMMERS, UNIFORM COMMERCIAL CODE (5th ed. 2000).

THE BUSINESS LAWYER, *U.C.C. Annual Survey* (annually in the August issue).

UNIFORM COMMERCIAL CODE LAW JOURNAL (four issues published annually).

UNIFORM COMMERCIAL CODE REPORTING SERVICE, CASES AND COMMENTARY (2d Series 1996 to date).

Revision of Article 2

Henry D. Gabriel, *The Inapplicability of the United Nations Convention on the International Sale of Goods as a Model for the Revision of Article Two of the Uniform Commercial Code*, 72. TUL. L. REV. 1995 (1998).

Henry D. Gabriel, *The Revisions of the Uniform Commercial Code—Process and Politics*, 19 J. L. & COMM. 125 (1999).

Gregory E. Maggs, *The Waning Importance of Revisions to U.C.C. Article 2*, 78 NOTRE DAME L. REV. 595 (2003).

Robert E. Scott, *The Rise and Fall of Article 2*, 62 LA. L. REV. 1009 (2002).

Symposium, Perspectives on the Uniform Laws Revision Process, 52 HASTINGS L. J. 603–701 (2001).

Symposium on Revised Article 1 and Proposed Revised Article 2 of the Uniform Commercial Code, 54 SMU L. REV. 469–1048 (2001).

Symposium: Consumer Protection and the Uniform Commercial Code, 75 WASH. U. L. Q. 1–672 (1997).

Linda J. Rusch, *Is the Saga of the Uniform Commercial Code Article 2 Revisions Over? A Brief Look at What NCCUSL Finally Approved*, 6 DEL. L. REV. 41 (2003).

Contract Formation

Robert A. Hillman and Jeffrey J. Rachlinski, *Standard-form Contracting in the Electronic Age*, 77 N.Y.U. L. REV. 429 (2002).

Daniel Keating, *Exploring the Battle of the Forms in Action*, 98 MICH. L. REV. 2678 (2000).

Christina L. Kunz, et al, *Click-Through Agreements: Strategies for Avoiding Disputes on Validity of Assent*, 57 BUS. LAW. 401 (2001).

John E. Murray, Jr., *The Chaos of the 'Battle of the Forms,'* 39 VAND .L. REV. 1307 (1986).

John E. Murray, Jr., *The Definitive "Battle of the Forms": Chaos Revisited*, 20 J. L. & COM. 1 (2000).

Daniel T. Ostas and Frank P. Darr, *Redrafting U.C.C. Section 2-207: An Economic Prescription for the Battle of the Forms*, 73 DENV. U. L. REV. 403 (1996).

Giesela Ruhl, *The Battle of the Forms: Comparative and Economic Observations*, 24 U. PA. J. INT'L ECON. L. 189 (2003).

Linda J. Rusch, *The Relevance of Evolving Domestic and International Law on Contracts in the Classroom: Assumptions About Assent*, 72 TUL. L. REV. 2043 (1998).

John D. Wladis, *The Contract Formation Sections of the Proposed Revisions to UCC Article 2*, 54 SMU L. REV. 997 (2001).

Contract Modification

Robert A. Hillman, *Policing Contract Modifications under the UCC: Good Faith and the Doctrine of Economic Duress*, 64 IOWA L. REV. 849 (1979).

Irma S. Russell, *Reinventing the Deal: A Sequential Approach to Analyzing Claims for Enforcement of Modified Sales Contracts*, 53 FLA. L. REV. 49 (2001).

David V. Snyder, *The Law of Contract and the Concept of Change: Public and Private Attempts to Regulate Modification, Waiver, and Estoppel*, 1999 Wis. L. Rev. 607.

Statute of Frauds

Michael J. Herbert, *Procedure and Promise: Rethinking the Admissions Exception to the Statute of Frauds Under Articles 2, 2A and 8*, 45 Okla. L. Rev. 203 (1992).

Scott J. Burnham, *The Parol Evidence Rule: Don't be Afraid of the Dark*, 55 Mont. L. Rev. 93 (1994).

W. David East, *The Statute of Frauds and the Parol Evidence Rule under the NCCUSL 2000 Annual Meeting Proposed Revision of UCC Article 2*, 54 SMU L. Rev. 867 (2001).

Jason Scott Johnston, *Symposium: Law, Economics & Norms—The Statute of Frauds and Business Norms: A Testable Game—Theoretic Model*, 144 U. Pa. L. Rev. 1859 (1996).

Frances Jan Malinowski, Comment, *The Use of Oral Admissions to Lift the Bar of the Statute of Frauds: UCC Section 2-201(3)(b)*, 65 Cal. L. Rev. 150 (1977).

Michael B. Metzger and Michael J. Phillips, *Promissory Estoppel and Section 2-201 of the Uniform Commercial Code*, 26 Vill. L. Rev. 63 (1980–81).

Robert L. Misner, *Tape Recordings, Business Transactions via Telephone, and the Statute of Frauds*, 61 Iowa L. Rev. 941 (1976).

Nicholas R. Weiskopf, *In-Court Admissions of Sales Contracts and the Statute of Frauds*, 19 UCC L.J. 195 (1987).

Deborah L. Wilkerson, Comment, *Electronic Commerce Under the U.C.C. Section 2-201 Statute of Frauds: Are Electronic Messages Enforceable?*, 41 U. Kan. L. Rev. 403 (1992).

Gary S. Fentin, Comment, *The Doctrine of Part Performance Under UCC Sections 2-201 and 8-319*, 9 B.C. Ind. & Com. L. Rev. 355 (1968).

Parol Evidence Rule

Lawrence A. Cunningham, *Toward a Prudential and Credibility-Centered Parol Evidence Rule*, 68 U. Cin. L. Rev. 269 (2000).

Peter Linzer, *The Comfort of Certainty: Plain Meaning and the Parol Evidence Rule*, 71 Fordham L. Rev. 799 (2002).

Michael B. Metzger, *The Parol Evidence Rule: Promissory Estoppel's Next Conquest?*, 36 Vand. L. Rev. 1383 (1983).

Eric A. Posner, *The Parol Evidence Rule, the Plain Meaning Rule, and the Principles of Contractual Interpretation*, 146 U. PA. L. REV. 533 (1998).

George I. Wallach, *The Declining "Sanctity" of Written Contracts—Impact of the Uniform Commercial Code on the Parol Evidence Rule*, 44 MO. L. REV. 651 (1979).

Unconscionability

Robert Braucher, *The Unconscionable Contract or Term*, 31 U. PITT. L. REV. 337 (1970).

M. P. Ellinghaus, *In Defense of Unconscionability*, 78 YALE L.J. 757 (1969).

Richard J. Hunter, Jr., *Unconscionability Revisited: A Comparative Approach*, 68 N.D. L. REV. 145 (1992).

Arthur Allen Leff, *Unconscionability and the Code—The Emperor's New Clause*, 115 U. PA. L. REV. 485 (1967).

Arthur Allen Leff, *Unconscionability and the Crowd—Consumers and the Common Law Tradition*, 31 U. PITT. L. REV. 349 (1970).

Carol B. Swanson, *Unconscionable Quandary: UCC Article 2 and the Unconscionability Doctrine*, 31 N.M. L. REV. 359 (2001).

Title

Grant Gilmore, *The Commercial Doctrine of Good Faith Purchase*, 63 YALE L.J. 1057 (1954).

Grant Gilmore, *The Good Faith Purchase Idea and the Uniform Commercial Code: Confessions of a Repentant Draftsman*, 15 GA. L. REV. 605 (1981).

Harold R. Weinberg, *Markets Overt, Voidable Titles and Feckless Agents: Judges and Efficiency in the Antebellum Doctrine of Good Faith Purchase*, 56 TUL. L. REV. 1 (1981).

Linda J. Rusch, *Property Concepts in the Revised U.C.C. Articles 2 and 9 are Alive and Well*, 54 SMU L. REV. 947 (2001).

Terms of the Contract

Randy E. Barnett, *The Sound of Silence: Default Rules and Contractual Consent*, 78 VA. L. REV. 821 (1992).

James W. Bowers, *Incomplete Law*, 62 LA. L. REV. 1229 (2002).

JOHN F. DOLAN, UNIFORM COMMERCIAL CODE: TERMS AND TRANSACTIONS IN COMMERCIAL LAW (2d ed. 1997).

Mark P. Gergen, *The Use of Open Terms in Contract*, 92 COLUM. L. REV. 997 (1992).

Victor P. Goldberg, *Discretion in Long-term Open Quantity Contracts: Reining in Good Faith*, 35 U.C. Davis L. Rev. 319 (2002).

E. Allan Farnsworth, *Disputes Over Omission in Contracts*, 68 Colum. L. Rev. 860 (1968).

Russell Korobkin, *The Status Quo Bias and Contract Default Rules*, 83 Cornell L. Rev. 608 (1998).

Brad A. Levin, *Applying the UCC's Supplementary Terms to Contracts Formed by Conduct Under §2-207(3)*, 24 UCC L.J. 210 (1992).

James J. White, *Default Rules in Sales and the Myth of Contracting Out*, 48 Loy. L. Rev. 53 (2002).

Performance or Nonperformance

John Elofson, *The Dilemma of Changed Circumstances in Contract Law: An Economic Analysis of the Foreseeability and Superior Risk Bearer Tests*, 30 Colum. J. of L & Soc. Prob. 1 (1996).

Larry T. Garvin, *Adequate Assurance of Performance: Of Risk, Duress, and Cognition*, 69 U. Colo. L. Rev. 71 (1998).

Sheldon W. Halpern, *Application of the Doctrine of Commercial Impracticability: Searching for 'The Wisdom of Solomon,'* 135 U. Pa. L. Rev. 1123 (1987).

Sarah Howard Jenkins, *Exemption for Nonperformance: UCC, CISG, UNIDROIT Principles—A Comparative Assessment*, 72 Tul. L. Rev. 2015 (1998).

Christina L. Kunz, *The 2000 Draft of UCC Article 2: Part Six on Breach, Repudiation, and Excuse*, 54 SMU L. Rev. 899 (2001).

Keith A. Rowley, *A Brief History of Anticipatory Repudiation in American Contract Law*, 69 U. Cin. L. Rev. 565 (2001).

Steven Walt, *Expectations, Loss Distribution and Commercial Impracticability*, 24 Ind. L. Rev. 65 (1990).

John D. Wladis, *Impracticability as Risk Allocation: The Effect of Changed Circumstances Upon Contract Obligations for the Sale of Goods*, 22 Ga. L. Rev. 503 (1988).

Warranties

Donald F. Clifford, *Express Warranty Liability of Remote Sellers: One Purchase, Two Relationships*, 75 Wash. U. L. Q. 413 (1997).

Jay M. Feinman, *Implied Warranty, Products Liability, and the Boundary Between Contract and Tort*, 75 Wash. U. L. Q. 469 (1997).

Harry M. Flechtner, *Enforcing Manufacturers' Warranties, "Pass-Through"*

Warranties, and the Like: Can the Buyer Get a Refund?, 50 RUTGERS L. REV. 397 (1998).

Michael J. Herbert, *Toward a Unified Theory of Warranty Creation Under Articles 2 and 2A of the Uniform Commercial Code*, 1990 COLUM. BUS. L. REV. 265 (1990).

Ingrid Michelson Hillinger, *The Article 2 Merchant Rules: Karl Llewellyn's Attempt to Achieve the Good, the True, the Beautiful in Commercial Law*, 73 GEO. L.J. 1141 (1985).

Thomas J. Holdych and Bruce D. Mann, *The Basis of the Bargain Requirement: A Market and Economic Based Analysis of Express Warranties— Getting What You Pay For and Paying For What You Get*, 45 DEPAUL L. REV. 781 (1996).

Sidney Kwestel, *Express Warranty as Contractual—The Need for a Clear Approach*, 53 MERCER L. REV. 557 (2002).

Curtis R. Reitz, *Manufacturers' Warranties of Consumer Goods*, 75 WASH. U. L. Q. 357 (1997).

William L. Stallworth, *An Analysis of Warranty Claims Instituted by Non-Privity Plaintiffs in Jurisdictions that have Adopted Uniform Commercial Code Section 2-318 (Alternative A)*, 20 PEPP. L. REV. 1215 (1993).

William J. Stallworth, *An Analysis of Warranty Claims Instituted by Non-Privity Plaintiffs in Jurisdictions that have Adopted Uniform Commercial Code Section 2-318 (Alternatives B & C)*, 27 AKRON L. REV. 197 (1993).

James J. White, *Reverberations from the Collision of Tort and Warranty*, 53 S.C. L. REV. 1067 (2000).

Acceptance, Rejection, Revocation, and Cure

Howard Foss, *The Seller's Right to Cure When the Buyer Revokes Acceptance: Erase the Line in the Sand*, 16 S. ILL. U. L.J 1 (1991).

Donald W. Garland, *Determining Whether a Nonconformity Substantially Impairs the Value of Goods: Some Guidelines*, 26 UCC L.J. 129 (1993).

William H. Lawrence, *Cure After Breach of Contract Under the Restatement (Second) of Contracts: An Analytical Comparison with the Uniform Commercial Code*, 70 MINN. L. REV. 713 (1986).

John A. Sebert, Jr., *Rejection, Revocation, and Cure Under Article 2 of the Uniform Commercial Code: Some Modest Proposals*, 84 NW. U. L. REV. 375 (1990).

Gregory M. Travalio, *The UCC's Three "R's": Rejection, Revocation and (The Seller's) Right to Cure*, 53 U. CIN. L. REV. 931 (1984).

Risk of Loss

Robert L. Flores, *Risk of Loss in Sales: A Missing Chapter in History of the U.C.C.: Through Llewellyn to Williston and a Bit Beyond*, 27 Pac. L.J. 161 (1996).

Margaret Howard, *Allocation of Risk of Loss Under the UCC: A Transactional Evaluation of Sections 2-509 and 2-510*, 15 UCC L.J. 334 (1983).

Remedies

Roy Ryden Anderson, *Damages for Sellers Under the Code's Profit Formula*, 40 Sw. L.J. 1021 (1986).

Roy Ryden Anderson, *Buyer's Damages for Breach in Regard to Accepted Goods*, 57 Miss. L.J. 317 (1987).

Robert Childres and Robert K. Burgess, *Seller's Remedies: The Primacy of UCC 2-708(2)*, 48 N.Y.U. L. Rev. 833 (1973).

Larry T. Garvin, *Credit, Information, and Trust in the Law of Sales: The Credit Seller's Right of Reclamation*, 44 UCLA L. Rev. 247 (1996).

Larry T. Garvin, *Disproportionality and the Law of Consequential Damages: Default Theory and Cognitive Reality*, 59 Ohio St. L.J. 339 (1998).

Larry T. Garvin, *Uncertainty and Error in the Law of Sales: The Article Two Statute of Limitations*, 83 B.U. L. Rev. 345 (2003).

Michael T. Gibson, *Reliance Damages in the Law of Sales Under Article 2 of the Uniform Commercial Code*, 29 Ariz. St. L. J. 909 (1997).

Charles J. Goetz and Robert K. Scott, *Measuring Sellers' Damages; The Lost-Profits Puzzle*, 31 Stan. L. Rev. 323 (1979).

Ellen A. Peters, *Remedies for Breach of Contracts Relating to the Sale of Goods Under the Uniform Commercial Code: A Roadmap for Article Two*, 73 Yale L.J. 199 (1963).

Richard E. Speidel and Kendall O. Clay, *Seller's Recovery of Overhead Under UCC Section 2-708(2): Economic Cost Theory and Contract Remedial Policy*, 57 Cornell L. Rev. 681 (1972).

William Louis Tabec, *Battle for the Bulge: The Reclaiming Seller vs. the Floating Lien Creditor*, 2001 Colum. Bus. L. Rev. 509.

ABOUT THE AUTHORS

Henry D. Gabriel is the DeVan Daggett Professor of Law at Loyola University, New Orleans and the past chair of the American Bar Association, Section of Business Law Uniform Commercial Code Subcommittee on Sales. A Commissioner from Louisiana on the National Conference of Commissioners on Uniform State Laws, he served on the drafting committees to revise UCC Article 2 on Sales from 1992 and UCC Article 2A on Leases from 1994, and from 1999 until their completion in 2003, he has been the reporter for both projects. He also chaired the committee to revise UCC Article 7.

Linda J. Rusch is a Professor of Law at Hamline University School of Law, St Paul and the past chair of the Committee on the Uniform Commercial Code of the American Bar Association, Section of Business Law. From 2000 to the present she has served as an American Law Institute representative to the Permanent Editorial Board for the Uniform Commercial Code. From 1996 to 1999, she served as the Associate Reporter for the Article 2 drafting committee. From 2000 to 2003 she served as an American Law Institute member of the Article 7 revision drafting committee and served as co-reporter for that project from 2001 to 2003.